Developing Resilience in

Developing Resilience in FE Teaching explores the essence of resilience and provides practical approaches for working in the Further Education sector. Emphasising the importance of reflection and self-growth, it outlines strategies to help teachers identify and deal with stress, using real-life case studies to exemplify key concerns.

This book is divided into three main sections: Part One identifies the sector's needs and recognizes resilience as a key attribute for FE teachers to survive and thrive in the modern world, explores the importance of strength and positivity in both physical and mental health, and examines the many ways in which these contribute to the development of individual resilience; Part Two outlines a variety of practical strategies and approaches for teachers to utilise their experiences to construct resilience over time; and Part Three presents real-life scenarios of resilience-building from various professionals working in the sector.

Developing Resilience in FE Teaching synthesizes a wide range of current ideas and research to provide a practical and useful guide for FE teachers, and for those working in the FE sector. It serves as an important resource for teachers and equips them with the necessary skills to become resilient professionals in the modern workplace.

David Allan is Reader in Further Education and Training at Edge Hill University, UK where he teaches on the PGDE in Post-14 Education.

Developing Resilience in FE Teaching

David Allan

Routledge
Taylor & Francis Group

LONDON AND NEW YORK

Cover image: © Getty Images

First published 2022
by Routledge
4 Park Square, Milton Park, Abingdon, Oxon OX14 4RN

and by Routledge
605 Third Avenue, New York, NY 10158

Routledge is an imprint of the Taylor & Francis Group, an informa business

© 2022 David Allan

The right of David Allan to be identified as author of this work has been
asserted in accordance with sections 77 and 78 of the Copyright, Designs and
Patents Act 1988.

British Library Cataloguing in Publication Data
A catalogue record for this book is available from the British Library

Library of Congress Cataloging-in-Publication Data
A catalog record has been requested for this book

ISBN: 978-0-367-42450-3 (hbk)
ISBN: 978-0-367-42451-0 (pbk)
ISBN: 978-0-367-82421-1 (ebk)

DOI: 10.4324/9780367824211

Typeset in Bembo
by Taylor & Francis Books

Contents

Illustrations

Acknowledgements

I would like to thank the following people for their support and encouragement throughout the writing of this: Mum and Dad, Tony and Alaina, my wife Venetia, and my children: Daniel, Jamie, Sophie, and Harry. I would also like to thank my commissioning editor Sarah Hyde for her patience and understanding.

Introduction

David Allan

In recent years, austerity in the further education and skills (FES) sector has resulted in many individuals working in challenging and highly problematic environments. 'The FE sector has experienced a prolonged period of reduced funding' (Hubble et al., 2021, p. 3), and education professionals in general have expressed concern, with over 60% self-reporting as 'stressed' (Education Support Partnership, 2020, p. 6) and as many as 70% having seriously considered leaving the sector at some point (National Education Union, 2018). Education is now identified as one of the key industries of public service where 'Stress, depression or anxiety is more prevalent' (HSE, 2020). Many teachers thus suffer in their professions and crave support.

This book is aimed at those working in the further education (FE) and skills sector. It is a guide for FE professionals for dealing with adversity and for emerging as a stronger and more-capable individual, ready to face the many challenges that working in FE can present. Its purpose is to equip individuals with the necessary skills to become a resilient professional in the modern workplace.

Most of us at some point in our lives experience stressful situations or face difficult decisions in our jobs. We may be confronted with challenges that seem insurmountable or be forced to deal with traumatic events that impact on our health. Whilst some people apparently sail through life without a care in the world, and seemingly exude amazing luck, the rest of us mere mortals are left picking up the pieces when tragedy strikes. Many of us fail to survive unscathed and thus need to nurse our emotional scarring. This book explores some of the factors those more fortunate appear to possess, such as the enviable ability to appear unphased in challenging circumstances and to effortlessly resume normality whenever the occasion calls.

Fortunately, resilience is not a characteristic we merely admire. It is a quality that we all have to some extent, and one that each of us is able to develop. It is not a magic ingredient of life, but it can have seemingly magical implications as it can transform how we think, feel and act. Whilst research tells us that we are born with some resilience, much of it is developed as we progress through life, experiencing the many difficult and often traumatic situations that modern living throws at us. Resilience, then, can be developed and it is the intention of this book to help you to do this, and to support you in not only surviving in FE, but thriving in it.

Resilient teachers achieve yet resist the compulsion to internalise pressures. They persevere in times of austerity. And they challenge unscrupulous workload demands and negotiate a fair and equitable system that promotes the triadic philosophy of good teaching:

1   The personal and academic development of students
2   The intellectual growth and professional development of teachers themselves, including the enhancement of their personal values and subject knowledge
3   The deep-seated commitment teachers hold of wanting to make a difference.

With rising levels of stress and anxiety in the sector, and the generally increasing problems in society that impact the mental health of many individuals (such as the current pandemic), developing resilience has arguably never been more important.

The book is structured into three parts. Part one explores the role of the individual, including the necessity for developing and sustaining resilience in the high-pressured world of the FE teacher. It examines the health and wellbeing of teachers and proposes resilience as a key combatant of both physical and mental ill health. Part two outlines a range of strategies that develop a positive approach to resilience building, including the development of confidence, self-esteem and autonomy. Part three emphasises the importance of reflection and self-growth and looks at real-life examples from the sector.

Building resilience can be difficult, and many of us fail numerous times before we eventually achieve. But perseverance is a key component of success, and developing resilience helps us to shield from adversity and continue until we reach the destination of our choosing. Fortunately, you have already made the first step on this journey as you are reading this book. Now, let us continue our quest.

References

Education Support Partnership. (2020). *Teacher Wellbeing Index, 2020*. Education Support Partnership. https://www.educationsupport.org.uk/sites/default/files/teacher_wellbeing_index_2020.pdf.

Health and Safety Executive (HSE) (2020). *Work-Related Stress, Anxiety or Depression Statistics in Great Britain, 2020*. Health and Safety Executive. https://www.hse.gov.uk/statistics/causdis/stress.pdf.

Hubble, S., Bolton, P. & Lewis, J. (April 2021). *Further education funding in England*. Briefing report. Number 9194. House of Commons Library. https://researchbriefings.files.parliament.uk/documents/CBP-9194/CBP-9194.pdf.

National Education Union. (2018). *NEU Survey Shows Workload Causing 80% of Teachers to Consider Leaving the Profession*. https://neu.org.uk/press-releases/neu-survey-shows-workload-causing-80-teachers-consider-leaving-profession.

Part 1
Resilience and the individual

1   The need for resilience

What is resilience?

'Barn's burnt down. Now I can see the moon.'

(attributed to Mizuta Masahide,
seventeenth-century Samurai poet and physician)

According to the online version of the Oxford English Dictionary (2021), resilience is defined as, 'The action or an act of rebounding or springing back.' To illustrate this, Lexico (2021) provides a range of interesting synonyms: 'flexibility, pliability, suppleness, plasticity, elasticity, springiness, spring, give, durability, ability to last, strength, sturdiness, toughness.' The ability to restore life to some form of normality after a particularly impactful upheaval is an important characteristic for teachers as they are often modelling good practice. However, resilience in teaching is much more than a retrospective approach to stress. Teachers are required to be prepared and thus exhibit signs of forthcoming resilience. This type of resilience is about having the strength beforehand to know that whatever happens you will try to cope. In this way, resilience is not immunity from stress, but the ability to cope with such stress in positive and productive ways (Zagalaz et al., 2020). This takes us beyond the use of resilience as a mechanism for resuming the status quo.

Resilience described as 'bouncing back' has also been criticised as it 'unrealistically suggests the absence of inner turmoil during this time' (Neenan, 2018, p. 2). In support of this, Gu and Day (2013, p. 26) state that resilience is 'the capacity to maintain equilibrium and a sense of commitment and agency in the everyday worlds in which teachers teach.' To go further, a review of the psychological literature by Färber and Rosendahl (2018, p. 621) noted that resilience is 'the term used to describe an individual's positive adaptation in the face of adversity, i.e. one's success in dealing healthily with significant stressors.' As such, resilience involves a form of 'successful adaptation despite challenging or threatening circumstances' (Masten, Best & Garmezy, 1990, p. 425). In this way, hurdles are overcome and risks are mitigated as individuals negotiate their way through various difficulties. At a more extreme level, challenges may pose a risk to health, wellbeing and/or general safety and thus require more severe

DOI: 10.4324/9780367824211-2

'survival' tactics. Resilience, then, is a characteristic that may help us wade through the mire of short-term difficulties but is also one in which life-threatening situations can be tackled through the biological response of fight rather than flight. Resilience is also a changeable characteristic, and its ingredients vary from person to person (Rutter, 1987).

Perspective

It may seem cliched to ask you to think about those people who have lost their homes and have continued optimistically, or about those who fought in a world war and so on. But at times this sort of perspective can help, particularly where these examples are taken from real life. We all have our own problems but in reality those problems are often small in comparison to the suffering of some individuals in this world. Moreover, it is often the individuals who have undergone much trauma who are the most resilient in life. As Morris (2004, p. 1) notes, 'Challenging times demand inner strength and a spirit that won't be defeated.' Through the use of perspective, you are not just comparing your life with somebody else's and saying 'it could have been a lot worse,' or, 'how lucky am I?' You are putting a context to your particular situation in order to frame your understanding. If you haven't suffered in the same way as these examples then these sentiments are probably true but perhaps difficult to accept. You may be of the opinion that this is your life, it is different, and what happens matters much more to you, regardless of how someone may trivialise the details. This is, of course, true. But what you can take from these extreme examples is the degree to which the individuals continued with their lives, refusing to give up. What compelled them to carry on? Where does that inner courage come from?

Resilience helps us to survive through difficult times and often when we are against the odds. From the Indonesian man who returned to the place where his house once stood – having now been destroyed by a tsunami – and said, 'Oh well, it's only a house. It can be replaced. At least my family is safe' before gathering whatever resources he could find to build a new home for his family, to 'Maria,' an incredibly strong Ukrainian woman who 'survived the Nazi invasion, the Chernobyl disaster and Soviet rule, and vowed to never leave her home' (see Flanagan, 2019), the world is replete with amazing stories of fortitude and resilience. Whilst these examples may situate our difficulty with some perspective, there is no getting away from the fact that what matters to us is what affects us, and even the most trivial situation can be overwhelming if we are not prepared. Just because we have not lost our house does not mean that we will not be stressed or won't experience real difficulty in coping.

The difference between acceptance and a realistic understanding

Resilience sustains happiness and helps us to accept that change is often inevitable, but that doesn't mean we should merely be content with a situation.

Developing resilience is also about resistance but accepting that bad circumstances happen to many of us is not quite the same as allowing these to impact on us. Resilience helps us to resist the urge to give up. It is our way of fighting through an event and eventually overcoming the difficulties. If we merely accept something, without challenge, we fail to utilise the power we have to make changes. But sometimes we need a realistic outlook, and having an approach in which we refuse to accept anything can be counterproductive. Take, for instance, the difference between the following two situations:

1   Your boss has been making unreasonable demands on you over the last two months.
2   Due to the low number of enrolments, the college has stated that your course will no longer be running and that you are to be made redundant.

A major difference between the two is the element of control that you have. You can mitigate the redundancy situation by seeking employment elsewhere, or perhaps if there are opportunities to teach across other programmes, but you may be limited in what you can do to change the situation. Some acceptance is thus needed that this will likely result in a change to your circumstances. For the unreasonable demands, however, you can demonstrate to your boss the impact this is having on your work; you can appeal to your boss's line manager; and, you can even make a complaint. You may not be able to cease the demands, of course, but you do have some pushback power. Both situations are not only different, the implications for each will vary, but a realistic perspective will enable you to identify whether you should challenge it or accept it and move on. Resistance is a strong tool in your arsenal but you should be aware of the impact it is having on your confidence and self-belief and thus act accordingly. Many people feel that resistance is beyond their power and that they have to yield. But if the stressor is placed into perspective, then a relevant plan for dealing with it can be devised.

Born to be resilient?

Fortunately, research tells us that resilience is not wholly innate; rather, it is perceived as a combination of genetic and environmental factors (Amstadter, Myers & Kendler, 2014). As such, resilience is an aspect of your personality that has been shaped by various experiences and this can mean that you are likely to be more resilient at certain times in your life and perhaps less resilient in others (Zagalaz et al., 2020). For example, the death of a loved one is a horrific event and is unfortunately an inevitable part of most people's lives. Some deal with this by showing strength of character and continuing with their lives, mourning when appropriate but also striving to function as normatively as possible. Often, having another loved one to care for encourages resilience through distraction. For some, however, the ability to cope in such situations is too much and merely drawing on one's inner resources is not enough to survive the ordeal.

But this does not mean that they lack resilience; rather, we all function within our individual constraints. Resilience is not an uncaring response to a fraught situation; it is surviving through adversity.

Although there are pre-determined features that will steer you in a particular way, and it is likely that these will regulate your general approach, it is also common for some people to demonstrate strong resilience in one day yet very little in another. In developing resilience, you are not trying to change an immutable characteristic, such as your height; rather, you are working on your mindset, your outlook on life, and your disposition. Your disposition can be difficult to challenge as it is to some extent ground into your character. However, you will have accrued a huge amount of learned behaviour throughout your lifetime and will be evolving regularly. Changing your disposition is heavily dependent on your situation and your outlook (indeed, it drives your outlook), and many factors can affect this on a daily basis. But resilience is something you can develop with practice. Practising to deal with difficult situations when they arise is a great exercise for developing resilience as it encourages you to avoid stagnating and can prevent the situation from exacerbating. It is not a substitute for the real experience, but when combined with reflective practice (see Chapter 9), it is a way for you to record the times when you have been resilient and why that may be so. Moreover, you are likely to remember those experiences if you have had to grapple with them.

As you can develop resilience, you may find it useful to tackle a situation in small steps. How you conduct yourself, how you approach a challenge, and what you feel inside are important factors yet, fortunately, within your control. But you have to be realistic in that this is by no means an easy journey if your resilience is historically poor, or if you typically struggle with increased stress and anxiety when faced with a problem. The problem may seem insurmountable (and some are, of course, and should be acknowledged as so), but categorising it will help as this will give you a realistic perspective of what you are facing.

Dealing with stress

Stress is a condition that you mostly absorb and thus place on yourself. For instance, if a deadline has been imposed on you, how you choose to perceive that deadline is up to you. Even though this is easier said than done, you can situate the deadline differently so that you are confident and prepared to tackle it, rather than perceiving it as burdensome and overwhelming. It is fortunate that you are not born with a limited supply of resilience because you can work on developing it. But this also means that you will have to work hard to do this if it requires a change in your outlook. Developing resilience will need to become part of your life and small steps are key; the first of which may be to place the stress into context. How important is this deadline? Is there a possibility for an extension if you are overwhelmed? Smaller stressors serve as a useful strategy for developing an approach to becoming resilient, and this can be used to tackle some of the larger stressors of the sector.

In 2018, the Institute for Fiscal Studies' annual report on spending on English education reported that since 2010, the Further Education and Skills sector has witnessed 'significant cuts to spending per student' (Belfield, Farquharson & Sibieta, 2018, p. 4). The sector has also borne out a comparatively poor rate of inflation for its teaching staff, despite the fact that 'Participation in full-time 16–18 education has more than doubled since the 1980s' (Belfield, Farquharson & Sibieta, 2018, p. 7). Moreover, measures such as the pressure to increase the sector's contribution to employment and the economy, the implementation of area reviews and mergers, changes to the funding for 16–19 students, and a general expectation to embed English and maths in most subjects can actively increase stress levels for both lecturers and students alike.

The modern teacher: Living or existing?

Today's world is driven by many social, cultural, and economic pressures that impinge on our professional lives and thus add to the existing demands of teaching. From the impact of technology and social media on the working day – with teachers taking home work-related concerns and struggling to switch off at a healthy hour – to pay freezes, disproportionate status across other sectors and general austerity measures within the FE sector that disrupt practices and impinge on motivation and enthusiasm; from the difficulty in engaging with students when (at the time of writing) the world is in the middle of a global pandemic and people are socially distancing to college mergers and job insecurity; from pressures to embed skills we may not have the confidence for (English and maths) to expectations that FE lecturers should engage with research as part of their professional development, the modern FE world presents many challenges for surviving in the profession.

For teachers, however, mere survival is inadequate as they must thrive. Teachers lead the way in their institutions. They motivate and inspire, they stimulate and incentivise, and they instil a passion for learning in others as they contribute to the growing autonomy of students. However, achieving this under a cloud of despair, attempting to appease bureaucratic bodies whose excessive expectations are both unrealistic and unfeasible, is problematic to say the least. Teachers are highly valuable role models in society and their prestige in England clearly needs to be better recognised. With this comes the necessity to demonstrate capability and resilience. But teachers need the capacity to develop resilience and they need the freedom to utilise the very skills they are expected to develop in their students. The capacity to role-model personal development and autonomy is essential, yet teachers can become more resilient when they have the freedom and support to do this. The task of growing resilience is a complex one and resilience is sometimes a characteristic we develop by challenging the status quo rather than accepting it. Developing resilience is also about reconceptualising the norm and refusing to accept unrealistic demands. It is about showing resistance to unproductive, and often detrimental, working practices and thus seeks to empower individuals.

Interdisciplinarity

FE teachers often work two or even three different roles and may even be required to demonstrate interdisciplinarity to accommodate these roles. Whilst some areas overlap – e.g. as a psychology tutor you may teach aspects of sociology or health and social care – there are pressures within many institutions for college staff to cover subject areas they may feel uncomfortable teaching. Whilst career expansion is a productive move, your resilience will either enable you to do this effectively or will signpost you in the right direction for challenging it accordingly. That is, unreasonable demands are unproductive and you should ask yourself whether this is a normal development of your role and skills, or whether you are potentially being exploited. This is, of course, complex and examples will never do it justice. However, if you ask yourself whether the adjustment is reasonable on both your behalf and the behalf of the college then it may take you a step towards deciding how you will handle it.

Resilience will support you in this in two ways. One, you take on board the extra demands and you even consider expanding your skills base and subject knowledge by agreeing to take on the role. Strong resilience is needed to put the extra workload into perspective but you tell yourself that this is an investment in intellectual capital that will benefit you in the long run. Alternatively, however, you may decide that this is an unreasonable demand. You will thus draw on your resilience to challenge the change and to demonstrate your worth in what you already do. The focus of resilience here is the strength of character that you need to resist the change. Resilience is a characteristic that helps us through change and we can see this clearly in the first point. But resisting change might, in itself, involve change if it is not something you normally do. If challenging the ideas of management is new to you then you will inevitably be faced with a change to your routine. Resilience will thus give you the confidence to do this as it is your ability to predict for yourself that regardless of the outcome you will be all right.

Stress and the FE and Skills sector

In recent years, the FE and Skills sector has become an increasingly stressful working environment for teachers, with '36,000 cases of stress-related ill health … reported each year' (National Education Union 2020). The University and College Union (UCU) has consistently found that large numbers of its FE-related members agree that their job is stressful on a regular basis (Court & Kinman, 2009; Kinman & Wray, 2013), and a potentially detrimental consequence of this can be seen through a more recent survey by the National Education Union (2018) which found that 70 per cent of teachers had seriously considered leaving the sector. The changes in recent years have been numerous; however, some of the more significant ones that call for greater resilience can be seen below:

- Extended and irregular teaching hours add strain to already-stressful roles.
- The requirement to teach subjects that teachers may not have been trained for can be disconcerting.

- Additional pressures to embed English and maths in vocational areas.
- A greater necessity to provide pastoral care and support for a rising number of students with mental ill-health, despite major challenges in the teachers' own abilities to be resilient.
- The need to embrace change (irrespective of how it impacts on roles) can be daunting for many.
- A growing list of administrative duties that are time consuming yet often not factored into a timetable.
- There is added pressure in adhering to all of the above under a cloud of recent cuts, mergers and redundancies that may have influenced many to seriously consider leaving the profession (if they have not done so already).
- Financial support: 'Further education colleges and sixth forms have seen the largest falls in per-pupil funding of any sector of the education system since 2010–11' (Britton et al., 2020) whilst 'In June 2020, colleges were left out of a £1 billion Covid-19 "catch-up" package aimed at tackling the impact of lost teaching time in schools' (Hubble et al., 2021, p. 29).
- Pay: Since 2010, there has not been more than a 1 per cent increase in this sector, with the figure for some years sitting at 0.2 and even zero. Indeed, *FE Week* reports that 'The current pay gap between school and college teachers sits at around £9,000' (Whieldon, 2021).

Colleges are under increasing pressures to meet heavy, top-down expectations, such as securing the highest qualification outcomes from young people and acquiring the most valued Ofsted judgements. This can impact on the quality of the teaching and learning process as a whole, although teachers usually avoid this happening by taking the brunt of the stress. In general, teaching today is a stressful profession but the environments FE teachers work in vary widely, with some healthy and productive yet others destructive and even health-threatening. In a report on teacher recruitment in 2019 by the Department for Education (DfE), it was suggested that 'The stresses of life as a teacher are increased significantly for teachers who work in less positive cultures' (DfE, 2019, p.11).

In 2020, the Education Support Partnership – which is self-described as 'the UK's only charity providing mental health and wellbeing support services to all education staff and organisations' (www.educationsupport.org.uk) – surveyed a variety of education-related staff through its *Teacher Wellbeing Index 2020*. Commenting on this, Sinéad McBrearty, the CEO for the partnership, stated the following:

> Workload continues to be a problem that can lead to talented people leaving the education profession: 63% of education staff have considered leaving the sector due to workload, whilst 53% reported personal mental health and wellbeing as a factor.
>
> (*Teacher Wellbeing Index*, Education Support Partnership, 2020, p. 3)

A report from the Health and Safety Executive in 2020 also stated that 'Stress, depression or anxiety is more prevalent in public service industries, such as education' (HSE, 2020, p. 3). With the current demands on the FE and Skills sector, then, many teachers are facing growing levels of stress and anxiety, but this situation is far from new.

Back in 2013, a study found that 75 per cent of FE teachers believed their job to be stressful whilst more than 25 per cent were 'exceeding the 48-hour maximum number of working hours stipulated by the EU Working Time Directive' (Kinman & Wray 2013, p.3). For some considerable time, stress has been a major component of regular FE teaching and workload has been identified as a major contributor (Ofsted, 2019). Indeed, teaching in general is said to make for a stressful career. The percentage of teachers who have seriously considered leaving the profession has been reported as consistently high for some studies – '57%' (*Teacher Wellbeing Index*, Education Support Partnership, 2018), '81%' (National Education Union, 2018), '65%' (Hays Education, 2020) – yet much lower for others: '20%' (Worth et al., 2015). In relation to workload, the *Teacher Wellbeing Index* (2020, p. 6) noted that,

> Nearly two-thirds (62%) of education professionals described themselves as stressed. Senior leaders experienced the highest levels of stress (77%). One major factor was long working hours, with 70% of senior leaders working more than 51 hours a week.

For teachers, the general role of teaching – supporting students from all walks of life – is highly rewarding, and this alone often keeps teachers motivated. Teachers continue to do what they are good at because they love the profession, and they love to bring out the best in people. Indeed, a high majority of teachers state that the reason for entering the profession in the first place was to give something back, and that something is the difference that they can make to others (Tang et al., 2018). Unfortunately, however, this is often superseded by pressurised environments and unrealistic workloads that drive teachers to consider alternative careers. Most teachers love teaching, they love to nurture individuals and are proud to play a significant role in their development. They are conscientious professionals who (mostly) aim to give back to society, and they certainly do not enter the profession for its wonderful remunerative packages. Most are happy to remain in teaching because they are passionate about it, but the administrative duties are often laborious and thus disincentivise many individuals.

In recent years, the DfE (2020) has aimed to reduce workloads for FE teachers through a range of strategies such as advice and guidance in the form of 'tips from school leaders' and a 'workload reduction toolkit.' The impact of this, however, is still to be seen and it seems that as this is mostly focused upon schools, many colleges are yet to be in a position to implement such strategies.

Impact on teachers

The impact of the demands of the sector can clearly be seen on the teachers as these are the professionals on the front line, dealing with the day-to-day teaching and student support which is the backbone of the institution. There is a powerful necessity, then, for FE teachers to build resilience into their working lives in order to cope with changes that are seemingly beyond their control. This is not acceptance, of course, as injustices still need to be challenged; rather, it is taking a realistic approach to the wider remit of the role. Moreover, this is also a feature of FE that is unlikely to change overnight. Many pressures emanate from beyond the institution – directives from the Department for Education, for instance – and thus are incredibly difficult to negotiate. The unhealthy number of teachers considering leaving the profession is a serious concern, and many of those who have lost faith in their roles are also feeling the pressure of the burdensome task of changing career, such as the costly and time-consuming investment of retraining. Where a teacher does leave the profession, an evident gap will emerge and this can result in additional pressures as the institution seeks to plug this gap by restructuring and subsequently shifting this workload onto other staff members. However, this can be the metaphorical petrol on the fire as those remaining are more than likely to be tired, stressed or even burnt out already.

Mental health and well-being are important in whatever we do, and many of the demanding roles we undertake are likely to generate health challenges. Our capabilities are constrained by factors such as time, concentration, social support, and previous knowledge and skills, and we can either exacerbate the situation or work to improve it. This is not to lay the blame on teachers, of course. Some careers do generate more-than-average levels of stress, and teaching is arguably one of these. But teaching should be situated within the wider context of the sector need, and the solution to dealing with stressors is not to merely toughen up and accept unreasonable demands. Today's FE teachers are under incredible pressures to meet incredible demands, and resilience-building is not just about coping in the environment. Resilience enables individuals to gauge workloads, to challenge unreasonable expectations, and to deliver a service befitting the professionals that they truly are.

References

Amstadter, A.B., Myers, J.M. & Kendler, K.S. (2014). Psychiatric resilience: Longitudinal twin study. *The British Journal of Psychiatry*, 205, 275–280. doi:10.1192/bjp.bp.113.130906

Belfield, C., Farquharson, C. & Sibieta, L. (2018). *2018 Annual report on education spending in England.* London: Institute for Fiscal Studies.

Britton, J., Farquharson, C., Sibieta, L., Tahir, I. & Waltmann, B. (2020, November 3). *2020 Annual report on education spending in England.* London: Institute for Fiscal Studies. https://ifs.org.uk/publications/15150

Court, S. & Kinman, G. (2009). *Tackling stress in further education.* London: University and College Union.

DfE [Department for Education] (2020). Reducing school workload. London: Department for Education. https://www.gov.uk/government/collections/reducing-school-workload#history

DfE (2019). *Teacher recruitment and retention strategy.* London: Department for Education.

Education Support Partnership (2018). *Teacher wellbeing index, 2018.* London: Education Support Partnership. https://www.educationsupport.org.uk/sites/default/files/teacher_wellbeing_index_2018.pdf

Education Support Partnership (2020). *Teacher wellbeing index, 2020.* London: Education Support Partnership. https://www.educationsupport.org.uk/sites/default/files/teacher_wellbeing_index_2020.pdf

Färber, F. & Rosendahl, J. (2018). The association between resilience and mental health in the somatically ill – a systematic review and meta-analysis. *Deutsches Ärzteblatt International,* 115, 621–627. doi:10.3238/arztebl.2018.0621

Flanagan, C. (2019, October 20). The Chernobyl survivors who refused to leave Exclusion Zone and are still living there. *The Mirror.* https://www.mirror.co.uk/news/world-news/chernobyl-survivors-who-refused-leave-20641627

Gu, Q. & Day, C. (2013). Challenges to teacher resilience: Conditions count. *British Educational Research Journal,* 39(1), 22–44.

Hays Education (2020). Staff wellbeing & Covid-19: Hays wellbeing in education report 2020. Hays Education. https://www.hays.co.uk/documents/34684/1181931/Hays-UK-Wellbeing-in-Education-Report-2020.pdf

Health and Safety Executive [HSE] (2020). Work-related stress, anxiety or depression statistics in Great Britain, 2020. London: Health and Safety Executive. https://www.hse.gov.uk/statistics/causdis/stress.pdf

Hubble, S., Bolton, P. & Lewis, J. (2021, April 30). *Further education funding in England. Briefing report.* Number 9194. London: House of Commons Library. https://researchbriefings.files.parliament.uk/documents/CBP-9194/CBP-9194.pdf

Kinman, G. & Wray, S. (2013). *Higher stress: A survey of stress and well-being among staff in higher education.* London: University and College Union. https://www.ucu.org.uk/media/5911/Higher-stress-a-survey-of-stress-and-well-being-among-staff-in-higher-education-Jul-13/pdf/HE_stress_report_July_2013.pdf

Lexico (2021). *Resilience.* Lexico. https://www.lexico.com/synonym/resilient

Masten, A., Best, K., & Garmezy, N. (1990). Resilience and development: Contributions from the study of children who overcome adversity. *Development and Psychopathology,* 2(4), 425–444.

Morris, T. (2004). *The stoic art of living: Inner resilience and outer results.* Chicago, IL: Open Court Publishing.

National Education Union [NEU] (2018). NEU survey shows workload causing 80% of teachers to consider leaving the profession. London: National Education Union. https://neu.org.uk/press-releases/neu-survey-shows-workload-causing-80-teachers-consider-leaving-profession

National Education Union [NEU] (2020). Managing stress and well-being in FE. London: National Education Union. file:///F:/Managing%20stress%20and%20well-being%20in%20FE.pdf

Neenan, M. (2018). *Developing resilience.* Abingdon, UK: Routledge.

Ofsted (2019). *Teacher well-being at work in schools and further education providers.* London: The Office for Standards in Education, Children's Services and Skills. https://assets.publishing.service.gov.uk/government/uploads/system/uploads/attachment_data/file/936253/Teacher_well-being_report_110719F.pdf

Oxford English Dictionary (2021). Resilience. Oxford English Dictionary. https://www.oed.com/view/Entry/163619?redirectedFrom=resilience#eid

Rutter, M. (1987). Psychosocial resilience and protective mechanisms. *American Journal of Orthopsychiatry*, 57, 316–331.

Tang, S.Y.F., Wong, P.M., Wong, A.K.Y. & Cheng, M.M.H. (2018). What attracts young people to become teachers? A comparative study of pre-service student teachers' motivation to become teachers in Hong Kong and Macau. *Asia Pacific Education Review*, 19, 433–444. https://doi.org/10.1007/s12564-018-9541-x

Whieldon, F. (2021, February 5). FE recruitment drive 'pipedream' without pay rises. *FE Week*. https://feweek.co.uk/2021/02/05/fe-pay-must-increase-or-government-plans-will-remain-a-pipedream/

Worth, J., Bamford, S. and Durbin, B. (2015). *Should I stay or should I go? NFER analysis of teachers joining and leaving the profession.* Slough, UK: National Foundation for Educational Research. https://www.nfer.ac.uk/publications/lfsa01/lfsa01.pdf

Zagalaz, J.C., Manrique, I.L., Veledo, M.B.S.P., Sánchez, M.L.Z. & de Mesa, C.G.G. (2020). The importance of the phoenix bird technique (Resilience) in teacher training: CD-RISC scale validation. *Sustainability*, 12(1002). doi:10.3390/su12031002

2 Teacher training in FE

Introduction

This chapter focuses on the difficult period of balancing study with work for trainee teachers as they juggle dichotomous roles whilst transitioning into the profession. It explores conflict and dissonance between the identities of teacher and student, and illustrates how it can be difficult to compartmentalise workloads. The chapter suggests that due to the intense nature of teacher training, trainee teachers need to differentiate between pressures in order to understand the wider role of teaching; however, it also argues that such demands are indicative of the profession today and thus an understanding of how these manifest, and are dealt with, is essential for developing resilience. A model of postgraduate study is presented that is representative of a typical teacher training programme for FE. This model is the outcome of several consultations with colleagues from HEIs operating similar programmes.

Undertaking a PGCE

Teacher training for the FE sector is widely varied in content and there are many routes that can be identified. Lucas et al. (2012, p. 677) point out that 'until the late 1990s the training of teachers in further and adult education (FE) in England had been the subject of little regulation by government.' Indeed, many lecturers came into teaching through vocational proficiency and thus learnt how to teach through in-service training. Teacher training today is clearly different, and a typical full-time model at postgraduate level (PGCE), with a duration of one academic year, would comprise an FE placement of up to three days and university study for the remaining two. Due to the Covid-19 pandemic, university learning is currently blended (a mixture of face-to-face contact and online delivery), and whilst college placements typically involve more in-person contact, there are expectations to support students virtually as well.

In addition to the full working week, PGCE trainees are also expected to produce academic assessments (such as written assignments), prepare theoretically underpinned lessons for their placements, and mark work for their own

DOI: 10.4324/9780367824211-3

students. To add to the pressure, many need paid employment to financially sustain them through the course, and this can be extremely demanding. Whilst there is often funding available for areas such as maths, science, engineering and computing, the sector is open to a wide variety of skilled professionals who will not be in this privileged position. Such valuing (and, by default, devaluing) of certain subjects can thus affect how some teaching roles are perceived.

Identity and resilience

According to Day et al. (2006, p. 7), 'Teachers' sense of identity is a major contributing factor to teachers' commitment and resilience.' Who we are, what we do and, in particular, how we do it is constrained by our resilience. We play many roles in our lives – professionals, parents, sons/daughters, friends, colleagues, committee members, amateur musicians or athletes, and so on – and these influence (and sometimes determine) our approach to tackling challenges.

Although our lives are often complex, it is perhaps useful to look at two aspects: personal and professional. In our professional lives, we can play a role and thus apply a little distance to a situation. If we can become more objective in dealing with it, we can reduce the emotional connection. Suppose you are supporting a colleague who is having problems prioritising deadlines. You may find this situation easier to deal with as it is non-threatening (i.e., it concerns someone else). This means it is less likely to 'trigger the so-called "hot," self-serving cognition that leads us to justify our own positions rather than seeking evidence that challenges our point of view' (Robson, 2020, p. 245). As such, the situation encourages us to make riskier propositions and thus expand our thinking when seeking a resolution. This is more difficult to do for ourselves as we often opt for the easy option because we think it is the safest, particularly when we can speculate the outcome. But having resilience can give us the strength to try something new with the confidence that if it does not work out in the way we intended we can deal with the circumstances. We often see this in teaching, where novice teachers feel inadequate and ineffective whilst more experienced ones grapple with motivation and commitment (Day et al., 2006).

Dual role

When training to be a teacher, regardless of the sector, you will find that your identity fluctuates between that of thinking of yourself as a student sometimes and a teacher at other times. This is perfectly natural but it can be difficult to reconcile as you also have your own students. Whilst it may seem to be a simple matter of switching from one to the other when the occasion calls, there can be difficulties in the overlap. One way to address this can be to fully embrace the role of the teacher, particularly as this is clearly where your career is now heading. This means that rather than attempting to resurrect your undergraduate self, engagement with your university assignments is perceived as 'professional development.'

Teacher training is unusual in some respects in that merely functioning as a typical student on other courses is fine and often expected. Teacher training courses, however, have different expectations of their students, such as teaching-related professionalism. As a student teacher, you may find that your identity is often in flux, and you may flit from one role to the other. However, you should remember that the ultimate goal is to enter the teaching profession and thus you will need to transition from being a studying individual to a working professional. Of course, in reality the world is complex and the two are not so clearly delineated. But for some perspective on the matter, it is a useful starting point for you to grapple with these concepts of identity. Unlike other courses, you do not wait to graduate before entering the profession, perhaps having gained a little work experience along the way. In teaching, you engage with your role almost from the outset through your teacher training placement.

As a trainee teacher, you will be required to be more autonomous and independent and under professional scrutiny. In placement, trainee teacher and teachers are often perceived in the same manner (particularly by students) as they are accountable for other people's progress. This can create additional pressures but good teacher training programmes will cater for the transition. It is important, however, that you understand your situation and how it impacts on, or develops, your resilience.

Using experiences to develop resilience

Having experienced an ordeal in our lives we are usually more prepared should something similar happen in the future. Part of our biological composition is to continue living until we have outlived our usefulness (nature does this by phasing us out through old age and passing on our genes to our offspring), and this means surviving our encounters and getting the most out of our experiences in the meantime. Threats to our existence vary, depending on our lifestyle, and many of us in the West are fortunate in that we do not face life-threatening situations every day. However, there are still many (seemingly mild) threats to our safety and wellbeing that we face regularly, and this paves the way for a natural necessity for resilience.

As humans, we have a natural compulsion to survive, and we need to tap into that at times in order to strengthen our approach when facing a challenging situation. Resilience helps us to cope in demanding situations, restoring our ability to function. From receiving a bill when we are financially struggling, and perhaps unsure of how we will pay it this month, to more immediate threats to our wellbeing such as the loss of a job, resilience plays a role in helping us to continue until such hardship passes. It is not unusual to find the small things in life more challenging, perhaps because we are not expecting them to be challenging. When faced with something like a life-threatening illness in a loved one, however, we already know it is going to be a long, difficult and emotional journey. Yet, we are sometimes stronger in these situations. In our daily lives, seemingly trivial matters can expand in relevance if we are ill-prepared, but this might also be a cumulative effect of pressures. A build-up of trivial matters can be overbearing because they grow in strength as they combine. Stress is pernicious and it is often difficult to avoid because we do not see it coming. Through experience, we can learn to identify the stressors, including the seemingly trivial ones, and thus prepare ourselves.

As a trainee teacher, and utilising your dual identity, you can distance yourself from the profession and observe the impact teaching has on experienced professionals, such as your placement mentor. As Johnson and Down (2013, p. 710) note, 'early career teachers are better placed both to understand the institutional and cultural conditions that have come to constrain them.' You can develop your resilience through analysing the behaviour and approach of those around you who are strong and seem to cope well in adversity. Through a vicarious approach (see Chapter 7), aim to identify the key ingredients of their professional outlook that ensure they are successful in tricky situations. How we view a situation can determine how it affects us; this is our mindset and it can determine whether we will be resilient or not.

Mindset

Dweck's (2017) mindset theory, despite having received its fair share of criticism (e.g. Chivers, 2019; Didau, 2015), is arguably a useful tool for developing perspective. We may not be able to change a situation, but we can change how we deal with it and how it affects us. In her theory, Dweck identifies two particular mindsets – *growth* and *fixed* – that we have when approaching an activity or situation. These represent our outlook and can be changed. Although the concept is a dichotomous one, it is not merely a positive outlook versus a negative one. Both can be positive and optimistic, and both can be negative and pessimistic.

In her book, which is highly accessible and user-friendly, Dweck outlines her theory of what motivates, and limits, many individuals when it comes to success. Based on her research in the field of psychology, Dweck suggests that we either exhibit a fixed mindset or a growth mindset. A fixed mindset limits our ability because we impose self-constraints such as, 'I'm no good at maths,' or 'I could never learn another language.' Primarily, we do this when we believe that skills and talent are innate and unchangeable. But this thinking restricts our potential, and those who adopt this mindset often fall at the first hurdle. Or, more specifically, they facilitate their own fall. This is not to say that genetics play no role in our abilities, however; rather, that our attitudes are powerful factors in determining our success, either inhibiting or facilitating our goals. A growth mindset encourages us to build on our resources rather than allowing them to constrain us, and our mindsets can evolve and improve as we become more experienced.

Mindsets can change for a variety of reasons, such as how well we feel we can deal with a situation and whether we believe that hard work can override talent. This links mindset to our ability to persevere through difficult situations; those with a growth mindset are more likely to demonstrate greater resilience (Yeager & Dweck, 2020). Your mindset is linked to your outlook and is based on whether you perceive intelligence to be fixed or believe that it is a malleable concept that allows for intellectual growth through determination and perseverance. As mindset is related to attitude, you might demonstrate either a fixed or a growth mindset, depending on the context. Of course, it is perhaps not easy to flit from one to the other as attitudes and beliefs are often embedded deeply within our psyche, but some areas lend themselves more to one or the other. As such, we can, in effect, display both a fixed mindset in some situations and a growth mindset in others. Raising awareness of these mindsets, then, can be extremely useful for changing our approach and thus helping us to become more resilient.

How does it work?

The growth mindset is about embracing failure as a mechanism for progress. When we fail to achieve something, we can either adopt the perspective that it was because it was beyond our ability, or that it will be possible to achieve it with much more effort. The latter approach demonstrates that we embrace a growth mindset: we are on the journey but not there yet (Dweck, 2017). More work is needed but we believe that the end goal can, and should, be achieved. With a fixed mindset, we do not believe that it is possible to achieve certain goals because they are beyond our ability. So why do some people fall into this apparent trap? The nuances of any approach can complicate matters because we know that some things do seem out of our control.

For the average person, it is likely that the possibility of becoming an astronaut and jetting off to space is improbable. However, whilst this might be a realistic perspective to take, it does not in itself preclude such an individual. Becoming an astronaut is a complex goal and requires around a decade or so of training and experience. This means that only a small number of individuals will choose this career path; however, it would be inaccurate to assume that only a select number of individuals are capable of undertaking this route, and that the reason millions of people choose not to do so is because they are not cut out for it. Putting aside some genetic traits that can put some people ahead of the crowd for certain activities – strength, size, length of limbs and so on – nobody is born to be an astronaut. This is an extreme example, of course, and you may well wonder what this has to do with working in FE (aside from teaching A levels to the next generation of wannabe astronauts). The point is that having a fixed mindset can limit your outlook and constrain your progress, thus making you potentially less resilient in the face of adversity.

The fixed mindset in action

Some people claim that we can be strong in either English or maths (but not both), and some have even progressed to state that this is a biologically determined factor. This is evidence of a fixed mindset in action. If you believe that you are not good at maths, it is likely that you will struggle with it as a subject. However, you may excel in maths in your personal life, such as calculating a percentage for a purchase or reckoning quickly what two-thirds of £118 is for an item in a sale. You may also understand how to calculate the cost of a carpet for your living room yet feel that maths is for other people. The fixed mindset can hold us back as we tell ourselves that something is not worth trying because it is too difficult to achieve. The fixed mindset can also stop us from progressing as we hide our weaknesses for fear of exposure. A student with a label of being clever, for instance, may find himself avoiding engagement with something challenging for fear of getting an answer wrong. This is a fixed mindset as there is a belief that getting the answer wrong means that the original label (clever) must be wrong too.

Individuals with a fixed mindset will refrain from challenging themselves for fear of failure, even though failure is an integral part of success. Great resilience relies upon previous failure because it is the experience itself that generates familiarity. As a trainee teacher, there are likely to be many areas that are still in development and this can impact on your confidence and ability. It is sometimes difficult to believe that you will get the teaching position you require if you have applied for several roles but not yet had an interview. Your experience of moving from job to job is perhaps not yet there so does not act as a reservoir from which you can draw. This is fear of the unknown and can affect your resilience as it impacts on confidence and preparedness. Whilst nobody knows what the future holds, of course, drawing on prior experience to make a plausible projection is resilience-building because it outlines possibilities we can utilise again. Experience thus acts as templates for the future.

In the fixed mindset, we struggle to improve because we believe that our current situation reflects our ability. 'I do not have a job because I am not cut out for teaching. Some people are born teachers so I can't compete with them.' In this way, our capacity to achieve is misidentified and we place constraints on what we will achieve. Having a growth mindset pushes us closer to being more resilient as it represents a 'try, try again, try harder,' approach. In the growth mindset, we conceptualise limitations as temporary obstacles. That is, we believe that we will achieve something eventually as long as we continue to put the effort in. The reason we do not speak that extra language we might like, or play that favourite musical instrument, is more often than not because we do not practise doing these things. This might seem like common sense – and arguably it is – but the fixed mindset is an easy one to adopt, where supposed talent overrides effort. The strength of the theory of mindsets is its simplicity. Becoming more resilient is about improving our approach to situations, and doing so requires us to change the way we react to these situations so that we are empowered and thus better prepared to handle them. Serendipity and nepotism aside, Dweck would argue that this is one reason why only some people reach the top of their game.

The fixed mindset and teaching

zIt has been claimed many times (albeit not robustly), and unfortunately by some teachers, that teachers are born and not made. This would suggest, of course, that teacher training is in some ways redundant. This is evidence of the fixed mindset in action and it has been shown to reduce resilience (Yeager & Dweck, 2012). Whilst it is true that many of your characteristics lend themselves to potential success in teaching – commitment to your role, a passion for your subject, a clear communicative approach, empathy, and so on – it is perhaps misleading to suggest that these have all emerged from your genetic predisposition to fulfil the educational development of others. Your experiences throughout your life will have shaped the way you are in a variety of ways and differentiating between these and your inherent traits can be a complex affair. On a simplistic level, this is the old nature versus nurture argument, and many have concluded, with an abundance of evidence, that we are formed through a combination of these factors. Indeed, resilience itself is comprised from the interrelationship between our genes and environmental exposure (Amstadter, Myers & Kendler, 2014).

It seems, then, that whilst we are born with some resilience, we continue to develop this through our experiences. To achieve this, mistakes in teaching should (where possible) be embraced. They should be utilised as experience rather than viewed as evidence that you are not cut out to be a teacher. You may have a longer journey than other people, of course, but this should not matter if you focus on your own development and set ipsative targets. These are targets that build on your current situation and are relevant to you. Ipsative targets decrease the urge to compete against others, particularly when the competition is potentially detrimental to your progress. A growth mindset helps in setting these as you accept that you may not be at the level of others but are confident that you can work at your own pace to eventually achieve an equivalence.

In sum, mindset is a theory that is in progress – studies are still being conducted to assess its potential – but, despite some criticisms, it remains prominent in the literature. For instance, a recent systematic review of studies into Dweck's mindsets suggested that 'The most commonly described learner benefits were that a growth mindset can reinforce a desire to increase resiliency and perseverance' (Wolcott et al., 2021, p. 434). Clearly, then, the concept is worth pursuing.

Box 2.1 Reflective questions

How does the mindset concept affect what you do as an educator?

- What is the impact of having a growth mindset on both you and your students?

- Can you identify any individuals you would categorise as mostly illustrating a fixed mindset?
- What strategies can you use to develop your outlook? How does this impact on your role as a teacher?

Visualisation

When entering the teaching profession, it is likely that you will have an idea of where you want to be in the future, and how you will gauge success. Success is a term that can be difficult to conceptualise as it can mean something different to each individual person. Success should be, however, the achievement of the aims you set out to do in your career, however small. This might be an aspirational vision, such as looking at a leadership or managerial role, or it may be that your goal is to secure a permanent teaching position so that you can excel in what you love doing. Having a goal, no matter how small, is a worthy investment and it will help you to structure your future in a more productive and worthwhile manner.

Whilst you cannot foresee how events will turn out, you can make plans and work on delivering those plans to the best of your ability. To perceive that your fate is merely in the hands of someone else, however, is somewhat akin to giving up. Although you will be dependent on others at times, such as awaiting the outcome of a job interview or promotion, you will need to play a major role in your own success. This may be through hard work (which can appear daunting if it is unfocused) and perseverance, the underlying factor that will ultimately determine your success. With perseverance comes flexibility and this is where you paint a realistic picture for your vision. To use the professional discourse on the matter, you may wish to construct your goals using a popular acronym such as SMART (Specific, Measurable, Achievable, Realistic, and Timely) or PACT (Purposeful, Actionable, Continuous, and Trackable). What is important is that you can identify realistic potential to achieve your goals.

Whilst factors may intervene to prevent you from achieving your goals, you have the power to circumnavigate these hurdles. Visualisation can help you to achieve this as it presents the future you wish to create. Let's take an example. You set a five-year goal to be in a permanent position in a college, teaching your subject area, and engaging in outside activities that are career enhancing, such as reading up on your subject, completing a master's degree or networking. What is the job that you want to be in? Your first step is to explore the job field now. You may not be in a position to apply for that job, but understanding the criteria will help you to identify what you need to work on to get there. Where are the gaps in your experience and what do you need to engage in so that you are in a better position to apply for this job and confidently present your case? Identifying this helps you to gauge just how far away you are from that role and will highlight whether your goals are realistic or not. Once you know what is involved, you now work backwards, devising your timeframe and generating your objectives. If this job is further away than you thought, then at least you are aware of this and can re-plan. Perhaps it is closer than you think, however, and you feel that you can easily evidence some of the criteria through the skills and experience that you have acquired through your teacher training.

Having a clear goal will help you to be resilient because it can keep you on track should you lose your focus. Having no goal is the metaphorical equivalent of a train running along a loose track with no end point. At some point it may derail or crash. But who knows when and who knows where? Your goals are your way of sustaining stability on the track. And your visualisation is your awareness of where the track leads. This is your professional life and the further you think ahead (if possible) the more you can guide that train. Having strong resilience will help you to be aware of potential faults on the line and can enable you to take evasive action. Moreover, if you should happen to derail, through no fault of your own perhaps, strong visualisation will guide you back on the track. This is resilience-building.

Resilience is important for dealing with those rejection letters (which these days come in the form of no communication at all − 'If you haven't heard anything in six weeks, please consider your application to have been unsuccessful'). At present the working world is a competitive one and this can impinge on your resilience reserves, particularly where you do not have a comparable situation or experience that you can use to situate your concern. Not getting the job that you want now does not mean that you will never be in that job in the future, of course, which is why it is important to establish your goals and then to keep pursuing them. Your visualisation will also highlight to you that there is an endpoint and this will help if you need to pursue an alternative route. Regardless of the hurdles you face whilst pursuing your dream, you can utilise your growth mindset by accepting that you are not at your endpoint yet but will reach it eventually (Dweck, 2017), as per your ipsative target.

Without goals, it is easy to become disillusioned and fall into a rut of low self-esteem and poor belief in your ability as a teacher, particularly if you find yourself between jobs. 'Perhaps I'm just not cut out for it,' you think, after your interview is announced as unsuccessful (even though securing the interview in the first place is a significant step forward in your career). Without goals, there can be dissonance between what you would like from your career and your actual trajectory because you have failed to map out an accurate route. Having strong goals will help you to challenge this dissonance because the structure you outline for yourself, your visualisation, will be able to manifest as a reality. Visualising where you would like to be and then setting small goals in order to achieve this can make your goals become a reality. This may seem cliched, but it is easy to fail to achieve your goals if you lose your focus. It is also easy to coast in your career because you cannot see that the route ahead is not taking you to where you want to be. This is fine, of course, if you are in a job you love, happy to remain until retirement, because in this way you have achieved your goal. However, even if you are comfortable in your role, you will still benefit from having a focus where your goals are centred on personal fulfilment within it.

Rejection builds resilience

Being unsuccessful in an interview can be disheartening but seeing the bigger picture is useful because it helps you to realise that that particular job is one of many. It is unlikely to be the sole route to achieving your vision, and getting a job in another institution can move your career forward in a very similar manner. This is resilience-building and often comes with experience and perspective. Two unsuccessful interviews after graduating can be daunting. However, two unsuccessful interviews against eight other interviews that you were successful in over your 30-year career paints a different picture. Success is what we remember and the more success we see the more resilient we become in dealing with the unsuccessful times and the rejections.

Visualising your goals will help you stay focused as you will learn to ignore, or discard, events that are not part of achieving that goal. Fixating on a job that you did not secure will do nothing for your plan. It is gone and you need to move on and there is probably little you can do. So why torture yourself? Why expend all that energy into what will NOT be when you can use it to focus on what WILL be?

References

Amstadter, A.B., Myers, J.M. & Kendler, K.S. (2014). Psychiatric resilience: Longitudinal twin study. *The British Journal of Psychiatry*, 205, 275–280. doi:10.1192/bjp.bp.113.130906

Chivers, T. (2019, August 7). The myth of the 'growth mindset.' UnHerd. https://unherd.com/2019/08/the-myth-of-the-growth-mindset/

Day, C., Stobart, G., Sammons, P., Kington, A., Gu, Q., Smees, R. & Mujtaba, T. (2006). *Variations in teachers' work, lives and effectiveness*. Research Report RR743. London: Department for Education. https://dera.ioe.ac.uk/6405/1/rr743.pdf

Didau, D. (2015, October 24). Is growth mindset pseudoscience? David Didau, Training & Consultancy. https://learningspy.co.uk/research/is-growth-mindset-pseudoscience/

Dweck, C.S. (2017). *Mindset: Changing the way you think to fulfil your potential*. London: Robinson.

Johnson, B. & Down, B. (2013). Critically re-conceptualising early career teacher resilience. *Discourse: Studies in the Cultural Politics of Education*, 34(5), 703–715. doi:10.1080/01596306.2013.728365

Lucas, N., Nasta, T. & Rogers, L. (2012). From fragmentation to chaos? The regulation of initial teacher training in further education. *British Educational Research Journal*, 38(4), 677–695.

Robson, D. (2020) *The intelligence trap*. London: Hodder & Stoughton.

Wolcott, M.D., McLaughlin, J.E., Hann, A., Miklavec, A., Beck Dallaghan, G.L., Rhoney, D.H. & Zomorodi, M. (2021). A review to characterise and map the growth mindset theory in health professions education. *Medical Education*, 55(4), 430–440.

Yeager, D.S. & Dweck, C.S. (2012). Mindsets that promote resilience: When students believe that personal characteristics can be developed. *Educational Psychologist*, 47(4), 302–314. doi:10.1080/00461520.2012.722805

Yeager, D.S. & Dweck, C.S. (2020). What can be learned from growth mindset controversies? *American Psychologist*, 75(9), 1269–1284.

3 Mental health

Introduction

This chapter focuses on the rise of mental ill health as a product of modern society and the pressures associated with working in the FE sector. It looks specifically at the impact of stress and anxiety on mental health and emphasises the importance of looking after our mental welfare.

Mental health is something that we all have and we should all take responsibility for the wellbeing of ourselves and others. However, the term mental health has been pathologised in many ways, and usage is usually attached to cognitive difficulties that would perhaps be more accurately termed mental ill health. Anyone can succumb to mental ill health and these difficulties can, and often do, arise through seemingly 'normal' lifestyles; for instance, where stress is a regular part of our day it becomes a pernicious threat. Maintaining good mental health is a crucial factor in building resilience as it is 'commonly considered a sign of successful coping with adverse conditions' (Färber & Rosendahl, 2018, p. 621).

Nature versus nurture

Resilience is formed from a combination of factors such as genetics and environmental interactions. The gene/environment interaction theory, which stems from the nature versus nurture debate, explores the interrelationship between our genetic structure and the environment in which we live (Crofton et al., 2015). Studies on resilience have estimated the genetic heritability factor as sitting between 31 and 50 per cent, depending on how resilience can be reliably measured (Amstadter et al., 2014). At least half of your resilience, then, may emanate from your experiences, which means that you have some control over how resilient you are. It is also useful to know that the remaining 31–50 per cent is not necessarily a limitation as gene behaviours can be influenced by factors such as environmental stimuli (Crofton et al., 2015). This means that you even have the potential to encourage your body to respond to stressors in certain ways that can bolster your immunity.

Improving your health and approach to work – engaging in a positive and enriching environment where possible – can impact on your biological resilience

DOI: 10.4324/9780367824211-4

(Feder et al. 2019). According to a study by Crofton et al. (2015, p. 20), 'environmental enrichment is a compound manipulation that provides a daily workout for the dopamine system.' This means there is much potential for using positive experiences to stimulate the mind to increase pleasurable feelings in times of stress. Positive experiences in this context would include stimulation through physical activity, social connections, and encounters with new and interesting challenges that are not overly taxing (stress-inducing) (see Crofton et al., 2015). The process is also cyclical. By becoming a more resilient individual on the inside, you exude a more positive approach on the outside, and thus deal more efficiently with the negative sensory input that can impinge on your health. Experiences thus buffer your stressors as you grow to understand better ways to handle them. In recent times, however, the societal isolation and individual working that has arisen form the Covid-19 pandemic has impacted widely on such environmental enrichment. This is discussed later in the chapter.

Stress

Wald (2015, p. 704) suggests that 'Resilience is defined as responding to stress in a healthy way,' and according to Xue et al. (2019, p. 131290), 'Stress can be measured in both physiological and psychological human responses.' Whilst stress is intangible, its effects are reified on the body. As such, it varies from person to person. Stress is thus the impact from how we perceive pressures. It is the effect that stressors have on our minds and our bodies, particularly when it is negative, and it is those individuals who seem to cope better who are often regarded as resilient. Some people experience the same stressors but are not affected in the same manner. These are resilient individuals, and interest in this area has been growing in recent years 'as a result of the observation of some individuals who remain calm under stressful situations where others develop psychiatric disorders' (Zagalaz et al., 2020, p. 2). This variance in resilience is important because at its extreme it can mean the difference between life and death.

'Stress is a killer'

Stress is the name we attribute to the accumulation of concerns in our lives that acts as a force on our minds and/or our bodies. It is defined by the NHS (National Health Service) as 'the body's reaction to feeling threatened or under pressure' (NHS, 2021), and Xue et al. (2019, p. 131289) state that 'prolonged stress may break the balance of endocrine levels, unbalance the autoimmune system and contribute to cardiovascular diseases.' Stress is a common feature in many countries (e.g. Benmansour, 1998; Chan & Hui, 1995; Zurlo et al., 2007). Americans have been noted as reporting some of the highest stress levels in the world (Gallup, 2020), while the situation in the UK is as concerning. A survey by the Mental Health Foundation (2018, p. 7) found that 74 per cent of its participants were 'overwhelmed or unable to cope.' Of course, Covid-19 has exacerbated these concerns in most nations, and its effects will live on for many years. But concerns over mental health were already gaining ground prior to its discovery. Stress can be a short-term condition and, biologically, it even has a useful purpose as it compels us to act and to overcome a challenge in a limited timeframe. However, the long-term effects are damaging and often impact on the health of our cognitive processing. As such, we should be wary of the effects stress can produce and aim to put our stressors into context.

In teaching, stress is the tension we experience when our workload seems unmanageable, and it can have a profound effect on our health and wellbeing. To counter this, we may need to adjust our attitude towards it. Attitude is significant for resilience as it can determine whether we feel equipped enough to tackle the situation (a bit like the 'fight or flight' scenario). This can be influenced through a rise in confidence and experience. As Rutter (1987, p. 316) suggests, 'High self-esteem protects; low self-esteem puts you at risk.' However, attitude can also be negatively affected, and Compton et al. (2016, p. 1) warn us that 'healthy attitudes and behaviors are often in danger of slippage due to exposure to social, media, and peer-group factors.' Sometimes, we cannot help but care because there is a seemingly heavy price to pay for ignoring the stress we are under – our job may be at stake, for instance. However, we need to consider the bigger picture as the workload will not reduce if we become unable to work, which is a realistic, and unfortunately all-too-common, impact of stress.

Dealing with stress

One of the difficulties in coping with stress, particularly when it is impacting on mental health, is that many individuals are faced with a variety of metaphors that are supposed to help them 'work through' the stress without ever identifying, and dealing with, its source. Phrases such as 'soldier on,' 'get a grip' or the gender-specific, and perhaps offensive, 'man up' have been used by unscrupulous managers in an attempt to reconceptualise the contributory factors as being self-inflicted or relating to characteristic weaknesses. Apart from the physical and psychological damage this can cause, there may also be consequences in the form of reduced resilience. In particular, mental health can often be viewed with less importance than physical health, and a study by the CV Library (n.d., p. 2) found that '63% said that they would feel guilty taking time off work for mental health reasons.' This perspective can be pernicious as the accumulation of mental health difficulties that people face daily can be much more severe than perhaps imagined.

Anxiety

Like stress, anxiety can cause problems to our mental health, particularly where the anxiety has long-term effects. Anxiety is a form of fear. It is nervous apprehension about a situation or event where the outcome cannot be easily predicted. Moreover, it is also concern that such outcomes may produce negative consequences. Building resilience through experience can alleviate anxiety as it can help us to make accurate predictions for the outcome of a situation. This helps us to prepare better, although it does not necessarily mean it will change the outcome. But preparation is key, and even when we know there will be negative implications to a situation it can still benefit us to have this information in advance so that we can build up some immunity.

The inoculation theory suggests that individuals can become immunised (or at least, more resistant) to forthcoming incidents by exposing them to diluted versions of situations that challenge their attitudes (McGuire, 1964). This is useful for resilience as it prompts the individual to investigate alternative perspectives and counter approaches. Experience can help to provide a form of inoculation as it can provide us with a blueprint for what is to come, thus reducing anxiety. In their study, Norris and Murrell (1988) found that those experiencing a flood who had also previously survived one were much more resilient. Arguably, these people had hope because they knew from experience that survival was a viable option. To replicate this approach in teaching, individuals might be subjected to mild and controlled increases in workload. Experiences such as redundancy are never pleasant, but their impact might be mitigated for someone who has previously undergone redundancy and is thus aware of the procedure. Experiences, then, can be resilience-building if they can inoculate the individual.

Anxiety can also be treated medically if it is a long-term concern. However, this step should be taken with caution for a variety of reasons. Firstly, medical treatment addresses a medical condition and anxiety can be temporary and thus may not require such treatment, although a general practitioner should be consulted for an accurate diagnosis. Secondly, anxiety is sometimes difficult to treat effectively. As DeBoer et al. (2012, p. 1018) note, the 'current gold standard treatments for anxiety disorders [pharmacotherapy and cognitive-behavioural therapy] are limited in their effectiveness.' It is useful, then, to try to get to the source of the anxiety in order to address it and comparing similar experiences in our lives can help us to deal with that fear of the unknown.

Resilience and depression

Crofton et al. (2015, p. 21) note that 'In humans, three of the hallmark symptoms of depression are anhedonia [difficulty in taking pleasure in something], social withdrawal and behavioral despair.' These three elements make becoming resilient a significant challenge. If we withdraw socially, and struggle to see anything positive or pleasurable, then we are likely to find it extremely difficult to believe in ourselves or to persevere through a troubling situation. Depression magnifies our problems and blurs our ability to tackle them. In normal circumstances, there are many activities that we can, and do, cope with. These are done almost without thinking because they are perceived as trivial – for example, paying a bill. Others may be more demanding, however, such as applying for a new job or moving house, because of the level of effort and commitment needed. With depression, even small tasks can appear daunting and this impacts on our resilience. When faced with more demanding challenges, it is easy to give up and allow depression to take control. This is obviously very difficult to handle and professional help would always be advisable. If possible, however, avoidance is the stronger option in the long run.

Depression and resilience work antagonistically. Depression can deplete resilience yet developing resilience is a strategy for alleviating depression. Resilient individuals can often deal with depression more effectively by persevering with their situation, even if the depression was brought about through the loss of a loved one (Fletcher & Sarkar, 2013). Resilience can stave off depression as it helps us to avoid focusing on negative aspects or areas of our work (or life) that get us down because we feel that there is no end in sight. In this way, individuals with strong resilience demonstrate greater optimism, a better ability to problem-solve, and effective stress management skills. Unfortunately, however, increased depression is symptomatic of the modern world, one that has been exacerbated by a global pandemic.

Covid-19

The recent global pandemic, said to have originated in late 2019 in Wuhan, China, has had a profound effect on most people's lives throughout the world. The following description exemplifies this:

> In spring 2020, people worldwide were forced to deal with the consequences of the COVID-19 pandemic, including loss of lives, quarantines, lockdowns, income cuts, and worries regarding personal health or that of loved ones. Stressful circumstances such as these are associated with psychological distress, declines in well-being, and the rise of psychopathological symptoms.
>
> (Brose et al., 2021, p. 468)

Covid-19 emerged suddenly and initiated panic and increased stress levels for many people, although some merely took the pandemic in their stride. A significant contributor of the negative reaction and rise in stress levels was arguably the unknown. It was not clear what impact Covid-19 would have on the world and this potentially heightened the fear, with some even claiming that science fiction was now turning to fact. Many people's lives changed dramatically, with perceptions of the virus ranging from disconcerting to traumatising, particularly for the horrendous death toll that ensued. For others, it was merely perceived as troublesome.

At the height of the pandemic, many individuals throughout the UK were placed on furlough as the country grappled with an enemy that was yet to be understood, and the government outlined intentions to return to 'normality.' Those identified as key workers – including teachers – were to continue in their roles but the landscape changed significantly. Teaching dramatically altered its form and colleges moved to a virtual learning model. The isolation brought about through a combination of national lockdowns and social distancing was a major concern, and the effect of this on the mental faculties of those involved is still being measured. However, early studies have suggested, as perhaps expected, that those more resilient among us illustrate comparatively lower levels of fear and stress, stronger coping strategies, and better sleep quality (Ahmed et al., 2021).

The importance of sleep

Many people are aware that cutting the amount of sleep they get each evening can be counterproductive and even give rise to serious concerns, but that does not mean that they will never do this. Think of all those late nights required to finish off your marking, or to prepare for the next day's teaching, merely because you have been frantically busy in the day. After finishing late and hurriedly sorting dinner, you realise it is now 9pm and you have yet to get to your marking. Aside from the lack of sleep that is clearly on the horizon, how productive will you be knowing the pressure is on and that you still need to be up at 6am to prepare for work? It may seem necessary to work late a few nights a week but what is the effect of doing this? Apart from putting you out of your routine, which is a crucial element of success, lack of sleep can lead to depression and excessive gains in bodyweight (Gomersall et al., 2015).

Balance and routine are essential for optimal performance for your mental faculties. Sleep enables you to have a productive day because it enables you to rest and recuperate. You cannot work hard, play hard, and sleep little without suffering the effects at some point. Whilst this might seem obvious, many of us ignore the signs and are still guilty of getting insufficient sleep over prolonged periods, a contributory factor of poor mental health, such as depression (Boyko et al., 2013, p. 3154). As well as a work–life balance, you also need to have a balance in your life of stressors and relievers. Stressors come naturally with high-pressured jobs, such as teaching, and often that means that they are difficult to control (Shively et al., 2020). Where possible, however, they should be counterbalanced by relievers. Relievers reduce your stress and provide an outlet for you to channel unwanted emotions and negative thoughts. Sleep is a huge reliever and getting enough is essential for you to function optimally.

Despite knowing this, it is surprising to see how many professionals work long and unsociable hours on a regular basis. Moreover, those with more stress in their lives, and higher demands on their bodies and minds, are likely to need a little more sleep than the average person. How much sleep do we need, then, if we are to shield ourselves from the effects of stressors? An exact figure for sleeping is difficult to give as there are many factors to consider such as lifestyle and age. According to Suni (2021), it is recommended that adults should not go below the seven-to-nine-hour quota. Even though there are remarkable stories of people surviving on four hours a night, it is usually the case that this catches up with the person at some point. A nap in the afternoon can boost you no end, but apart from the fact that it is highly impractical in your line of work, it may steer you towards developing a poor routine and going to bed later than usual by way of compensation.

To balance your stressors and relievers, you first need to categorise them and then rank them. For example, sleep is a reliever but it only ranks highly when it is regular and of a good quality. It is hard to feel resilient when you are tired because drowsiness prepares your body to yield. Resilience sometimes involves fighting on, working through difficult times, with minimum detriment; but people who are regularly tired struggle to maintain this fight. Drowsiness is distracting and unproductive and humans need regulation. We have evolved to align with the earth's day and night timeframe and drowsiness provides a natural end to the day when your body is closing down. At this stage in the day, your body naturally wants to slow down to prepare for sleep. These signals alert us to the fact that our best performance is likely to be earlier in the day. Of course, this is based on the average person and you will know your body best.

To be drowsy in the day suggests that you are out of sync in your alertness–drowsiness cycle and this is likely due to your extended working day and thus lack of opportunity to relax. You may also find that you are overly active in the evenings. If you are getting your quota of sleep yet still feel tired, you may need to explore the quality of your sleep. Eight hours of broken and restless sleep can be less productive than a continuous seven-hour block.

What makes good-quality sleep?

If you are suffering with stress as a result of your workload, this will probably impact on your sleeping patterns. Whilst the simplest method of resolving this is to address the stressor – that is, to reduce your workload – this is not always possible so you may have to find an alternative approach. One strategy would be to set yourself a time that you will finish each day. Your working day probably varies but having a cut-off point will help you to compartmentalise your day. This will enable you to have some time in the evening to relax. To achieve this, you will need to plan effectively and adhere to this plan firmly. Unfinished business will probably circulate in your head, of course, so you may have to practise shutting it out. Achieving closure is difficult but you can produce a to-do list just before you finish for the day that can be picked up the next day. In this way, your thoughts can be transferred to the page, allowing you to relax. This is particularly important if you are working from home where the boundaries of your work–home situation can appear nebulous.

Without sufficient sleep your mood and attitude may deteriorate. Sleep is an important aspect of health yet, as argued, is often overlooked. The signs of sleep deprivation are varied – e.g. mouth ulcers, acne, lethargy, and poor motivation – but it is easy to diagnose if you know what to look for. And when your body is under stress, you may even need more sleep than usual. Sleep also affords the brain an opportunity to process the day's events, helping us to reflect more efficiently. Our bodies sometimes need more sleep when we exercise because our muscles need to recuperate (see Chapter 4). This illustrates the cyclical effect of stress and rest. The more we tax our minds and our bodies, the less efficient we are in functioning, which means we will achieve much less and our attitudes will deteriorate. We may feel the urge to stay awake longer to finish off that marking or to meet that deadline; however, if staying up for another three hours to work is comparable in efficiency to, say, 30 minutes' productivity then was there really any point?

Circadian rhythms

According to Suni (2020), our circadian rhythms are the '24-hour cycles that are part of the body's internal clock, running in the background to carry out essential functions and processes.' The word 'circadian' refers to the period to which we align ourselves; namely, our day. This is the routine that humans follow and for which we seem to have evolved. It is our natural structure and falling out of it has been linked with depression and other mood disorders (Germain & Kupfer, 2008).

The terms diurnal and nocturnal refer to activities that either take place during the day or at night, respectively. Humans are diurnal creatures, operating in the day and resting in the night. Our bodies respond to daylight, and we feel fresh and ready to tackle the day more when we are out in the sunshine. (This is one reason why looking at your mobile phone keeps you awake at night. The light on the phone tricks your brain into thinking it is daytime.) In the evening, we naturally begin to wind down as darkness draws in and our levels of melatonin increase. This is nature's way of saying that we must rest soon and prepare for the next day, and it is clear from this that routine is an important biological factor in how well we function. This affects productivity too and can either lay a strong foundation for success or raise many challenges for us to overcome – such as continual tiredness, apathy, poor motivation and even low self-esteem – as we lose faith in our ability to achieve.

Functioning strongly in the day and resting in the night is what most of us would consider to be the norm. This is the optimal cycle you can have as it follows nature's lead; however, not everybody has the luxury of falling in line with this template and many professions, such as emergency work, involve a nocturnal routine as they involve shift work – regular patterns of working through the night. This presents a challenge to both the body and the mind and requires much resilience and many lifestyle adjustments to cope with it. As teachers, we are fortunate to be able to follow a diurnal routine and should thus utilise it well.

Box 3.1 Strategies for a good night's sleep

- **Cut down on caffeine**. A study by Drake et al. (2013) showed that caffeine can disrupt sleep even when taken 6 hours before bedtime. We all feel that we need a boost at times but for those who cannot function without their morning coffee it is useful to know that after a while of using caffeine in this way its stimulant effect reduces significantly.
- **Take a warm bath.** This can prepare your body for rest.
- **Subdue your lighting.** Avoid looking at your phone.
- **Read, rather than watch TV, before you go to sleep.**
- **Eat a healthy diet**. Some foods make you sluggish whilst others are more energy-inducing (see Chapter 4).
- **Draw up a list for the next day**. You can address your concerns when you have a clearer head
- **Listen to soothing music (low volume and preferably no lyrics)**. The low volume is important because as you settle it will appear to grow louder. This is because you filter out extraneous sounds as you focus on the music.
- **Consider supplements** – some experts claim that supplements are unnecessary when you have a good clean diet, whereas others suggest there is nothing wrong with a little insurance. Low levels of iron and some of the B vitamin family can zap you of your natural pep, so if this is a long-term problem you may wish to seek dietary advice or speak to your doctor for testing.

Belonging: The importance of connecting with others

Do you find that you are less stressed when surrounded by like-minded people? According to Aguilar (2018, p. 29), your sociopolitical identity – 'the social groups to which you belong' – can play a role in determining the level of stress you feel in a situation. This is because 'your values and beliefs are cultural constructs.' Sharing a space with others who hold the same values as you can be soothing as there is less conflict of opinion. In times of significant stress in your life, this is often a necessity, at least until you are feeling stronger and ready to handle the world. Once you are stronger, however, you should challenge yourself by interacting with those who can offer constructive feedback on your teaching approach. In this way, you might even be called upon to question your values or to think in a different way. Learning is effective when it challenges us but it can become somewhat of a threat. This is positive as it means we are stretching ourselves and it sends a message to our brains that this information is significant. This does not mean that you have to accept what your colleagues say, of course, and engaging in a debate might result in you reaffirming your prior beliefs. But this will mean that your beliefs are potentially robust as they have been subjected to scrutiny.

Surrounding yourself in an echo chamber in your job can stymy your intellectual growth (Robson, 2020), and this seems an unusual strategy for an educator. But many teachers like to liaise with someone who complements their thinking. Growing your self-knowledge and self-awareness, however, can help to identify your biases and turn these into strengths (Aguilar, 2018). Working collaboratively is thus beneficial for your development as a teacher because your colleagues can validate and/or critique your ideas. As such, you should broaden your interactions to include both colleagues who are supportive (particularly when lacking confidence) and, when you are feeling more resilient, colleagues who provide a realistic reflection of who you are. Whilst you are unlikely to benefit from aggressive conflict, a little challenging at times is healthy and will enable you to develop your resilience.

Being aware of your identity is a powerful tool in your arsenal for how you interact with others and for understanding how and why things trigger stress and anxiety for you. There may be a work colleague you wish to avoid because he is deliberately provocative. But it is useful to analyse such interactions to understand what role you play in this. For instance, are you being intolerant and unwilling to accept that other people have views and values that may not align with yours? Or do you embrace difference and accept that not everyone will think, or indeed look, like you? This is easier said than done and most of us are comfortable in our beliefs that we are tolerant and accepting. Some argue that the word tolerant is unfortunate because it suggests that you have to be willing to accept the differences of other people, as if they are deviating from the norm and you are therefore allowing this to happen. However, tolerance is arguably the correct term for this behaviour because anything and anyone that is different from yourself is, in some ways, deviating from a norm. This norm is the one you have set yourself and it is one that you use to judge others. And those people will also have their own norms that you may fail to fit.

Tolerance, therefore, is key because you are right to have your views and values and have every right to hold onto these. However, there needs to be an acceptance that others will challenge these values without necessarily being wrong. And, of course, because your values conflict with others that does not necessarily make you wrong (extremist behaviours aside, of course). When there is conflict there is often a clash of values and this can be stress-inducing, particularly if we are in the minority. Self-awareness helps us to understand those values so that we can put them into context and learn to live in complex situations without unnecessary stress.

Connecting with others is essential for building confidence and developing professionally. Human connections are essential for us to form a healthy attitude. Surrounding yourself with like-minded people will help to build your confidence, but you should also engage with people of different beliefs, values, and opinions as this challenge can offer more long-term benefits for your development, such as expanding your ideas on resilience as you reflect on your attitude and situation.

Positive emotions

Barbara Fredrickson's (1998) broaden-and-build theory centres on the influence positive emotions can have on our approach to dealing with a situation. She argues that they 'produce optimal functioning' (Fredrickson, 2004, p. 1367) and can therefore facilitate efficient cognitive processes. Experiencing such emotions can generate greater resiliency as we form a more structured and efficient plan of defence when faced with a stressful ordeal. This effect is in some ways limited – for instance, 'positive emotions seldom occur in life-threatening situations' (Fredrickson, 2004, p. 1369) – but it does promote our ability to absorb problems as a teacher.

Teachers who experience more negative emotions than positive ones may worry unnecessarily because their thinking is focused on the harmful effects of a possible outcome. For instance, we may believe that the majority of our students are going to fail this year. This is a serious concern but we first need to make an accurate assessment of it. We may be facing a potentially stressful situation in that our position is under threat and this can impact on our mental health. However, we should question the evidence we have for this claim and ask if the situation could change. We can also deal with this productively by employing positive emotions; for instance, continuing to support the students and aiming to mitigate the impact. Our energy is much more efficacious, then, if it is centred on what is within our capability to change. We may not be able to control the situation but we can control how it affects us. Whilst clear thinking and reflection is essential, worrying will likely cause unnecessary stress. Positive emotions provide a buffer for surviving a traumatic experience, and when we draw on these we become open to possible solutions. Negative emotions, however, are detrimental to healthy cognitive functioning and they hinder us from thinking clearly, thus preventing us from engendering a resolution.

References

Aguilar, E. (2018). *Onward: Cultivating emotional resilience in educators.* Hoboken, NJ: Jossey-Bass.

Ahmed, O., Hossain, K.N., Siddique, R.F. & Jobe, M.C. (2021). COVID-19 fear, stress, sleep quality and coping activities during lockdown, and personality traits: A person-centered approach analysis. *Personality and Individual Differences*, 178, 1–7. https://doi.org/10.1016/j.paid.2021.110873

Amstadter, A.B., Myers, J.M. & Kendler, K.S. (2014). Psychiatric resilience: Longitudinal twin study. *The British Journal of Psychiatry*, 205, 275–280. doi:10.1192/bjp.bp.113.130906

Benmansour, N. (1998). Job satisfaction, stress and coping strategies among Moroccan high school teachers. *Mediterranean Journal of Educational Studies*, 3, 13–33.

Boyko, E.J., Seelig, A.D., Jacobson, I.G., Hooper, T.I., Smith, B. & Smith, T.C. (2013). Sleep characteristics, mental health, and diabetes risk: A prospective study of U.S. military service members in the millennium cohort study. *Diabetes Care*, 36, 3154–3161. http://dx.doi.org.edgehill.idm.oclc.org/10.2337/dc13-0042

Brose, A., Blanke, E.S., Schmiedek, F., Kramer, A.C., Schmidt, A. & Neubauer, A.B. (2021). Change in mental health symptoms during the COVID-19 pandemic: The role of appraisals and daily life experiences. *Journal of Personality*, 89, 468–482.

Chan, D.W. & Hui, E.K.P. (1995). Burnout and coping among Chinese secondary school teachers in Hong Kong. *British Journal of Educational Psychology*, 65, 15–25.

Compton. J., Jackson. B. & Dimmock, J.A. (2016). Persuading others to avoid persuasion: Inoculation theory and resistant health attitudes. *Frontiers in Psychology*, 7 (122), 1–9.

Crofton, E.J., Zhang, Y. & Green, T.A. (2015). Inoculation stress hypothesis of environmental enrichment. *Neuroscience and Biobehavioral Reviews*, 49, 19–31. doi:10.1016/j.neubiorev.2014.11.017

CV Library (n.d.) *Mental health in the workplace*. CV Library. https://www.cv-library.co.uk/recruitment-insight/wp-content/uploads/2017/11/CVL_MentalHealthWorkplace_Report.pdf

DeBoer, L.B., Powers, M.B., Utschig, A.C., Otto, M.W. & Smits, J.A.J. (2012). Exploring exercise as an avenue for the treatment of anxiety disorders. *Expert Review of Neurotherapeutics*, 12(8), 1011–1022. doi:10.1586/ern.12.73

Drake, C., Roehrs, T., Shambroom, J. & Roth, T. (2013). Caffeine effects on sleep taken 0, 3, or 6 hours before going to bed. *Journal of Clinical Sleep Medicine*, 9(11), 1195–1200. https://doi.org/10.5664/jcsm.3170

Färber, F. & Rosendahl, J. (2018). The association between resilience and mental health in the somatically ill – a systematic review and meta-analysis. *Deutsches Ärzteblatt International*, 115, 621–627. doi:10.3238/arztebl.2018.0621

Feder, A., Fred-Torres, S., Southwick, S.M. & Charney, D.S. (2019). The biology of human resilience: Opportunities for enhancing resilience across the life span. *Biological Psychiatry*, 86, 443–453.

Fletcher, D. & Sarkar, M. (2013). Psychological resilience: A review and critique of definitions, concepts, and theory. *European Psychologist*, 18(1), 12–23. doi:10.1027/1016–9040/a000124

Fredrickson, B.L. (1998). What good are positive emotions? *Review of General Psychology*, 2(3), 300–319.

Fredrickson, B.L. (2004). The broaden-and-build theory of positive emotions. *Philosophical Transactions of the Royal Society of London, Series B: Biological Sciences*, 359(1449), 1367–1377.

Gallup (2020). *Global emotions report*. Gallop Inc. https://www.gallup.com/analytics/349280/gallup-global-emotions-report.aspx

Germain, A. & Kupfer, D.J. (2008). Circadian rhythm disturbances in depression. *Human Psychopharmacology*, 23, 571–585. doi:10.1002/hup.964

Gomersall, S.R., Nortonc, K., Maher, C., English, C. & Olds, T.S. (2015). In search of lost time: When people undertake a new exercise program, where does the time come from? A randomized controlled trial. *Journal of Science and Medicine in Sport*, 18, 43–48.

McGuire, W.J. (1964). Inducing resistance to persuasion: Some contemporary approaches. In L. Berkowitz (Ed.), *Advances in experimental social psychology* (pp. 191–229). London: Academic Press.

Mental Health Foundation (2018). Stress: Are we coping? Mental Health Foundation https://www.mentalhealth.org.uk/sites/default/files/stress-are-we-coping.pdf

NHS (2021). Feeling stressed. National Health Service. https://www.nhs.uk/every-mind-matters/mental-health-issues/stress/#what-is

Norris, F.H. & Murrell, S.A. (1988). Prior experience as a moderator of disaster impact on anxiety symptoms in older adults. *American Journal of Community Psychology*, 16, 665–683.

Robson, D. (2020). *The intelligence trap.* London: Hodder & Stoughton.

Rutter, M. (1987). Psychosocial resilience and protective mechanisms. *American Journal of Orthopsychiatry*, 57(3), 316–331.

Shively, C.A., Appt, S.E., Chen, H., Day, S.M., Frye, B.M., Shaltout, H.A., Silverstein-Metzler, M.G., Snyder-Mackler, N., Uberseder, B., Vitolins, M.Z. & Register, T.C. (2020). Mediterranean diet, stress resilience, and aging in nonhuman primates. *Neurobiology of Stress*, 13, 1–10. https://doi.org/10.1016/j.ynstr.2020.100254

Suni, E. (2020, September 25). Circadian rhythm. Sleep Foundation. https://www.sleep foundation.org/circadian-rhythm

Suni, E. (2021, March 10). How much sleep do we really need? Sleep Foundation. http s://www.sleepfoundation.org/how-sleep-works/how-much-sleep-do-we-really-need#:~:text=National%20Sleep%20Foundation%20guidelines1,to%208%20hours%20per%20night

Xue, M., Liang, R.H., Yu, B., Funk, M., Hu, J. & Feijs, L. (2019). AffectiveWall: Designing collective stress-related physiological data visualization for reflection. *IEEE Access*, 7(10), 131289–131303. doi:10.1109/ACCESS.2019.2940866

Wald, H.S. (2015). Professional identity (trans)formation in medical education. *Academic Medicine*, 90(6), 701–706. doi:10.1097/ACM.0000000000000731

Zagalaz, J.C., Manrique, I.L., Veledo, M.B.S.P., Sánchez, M.L.Z & de Mesa, C.G.G. (2020). The importance of the phoenix bird technique (Resilience) in teacher training: CD-RISC scale validation. *Sustainability*, 12(1002). doi:10.3390/su12031002

Zurlo, M.C., Pes, D. & Cooper, C.L. (2007). Stress in teaching: A study of occupational stress and its determinants among Italian schoolteachers. *Stress and Health*, 23, 231–241. doi:10.1002/smi.1141

4   Physical health

'Most people die at 25 and aren't buried until they're 75.'

(attributed to Benjamin Franklin)

Introduction

In this chapter, the importance of physical health is explored, particularly in relation to exercise and its effect on outlook. The health effects of work pressures within FE are examined, and a healthy work–life balance is advocated. The chapter also considers the biological benefits of exercise,[1] such as how it can stabilise moods and promote a healthy outlook to teaching, as well as its importance in regulating our lifestyles. Both physical health and mental health are heavily interrelated and the maintenance of each is essential for optimal resilience. Your physical health plays a key role in how you cope in times of difficulty because a healthy body is a strong contributory factor for a healthy mind. Achieving this whilst meeting the many demands of teaching, however, requires strategic planning, strong commitment, and plain determination.

Physical health

Many of us imagine ourselves to be physically healthy. Indeed, if we compare ourselves to those less active than us, we may feel that we are ahead of the game. But achieving good physical health means much more than engaging in regular movement. As an FE teacher, you are likely to be quite active throughout the day, but to what extent is this contributing to your overall health? Achieving good physical health relies on a variety of factors, and if any one of these is neglected it can be counterproductive for both your physical and mental health. Recuperation, for instance, is essential for developing your ability to tackle those heavy workloads; yet, it is often difficult to fit this in when there are several deadlines to meet, classes to teach, and student concerns to resolve. As teachers, we are often tempted to continue through difficult times because this is 'just what we do.' We may even feel that doing so will develop our resilience. However, this can damage our resilience as it will likely wear us down physically and impact on our attitude. Achieving good physical

DOI: 10.4324/9780367824211-5

health often requires some form of movement in order to encourage our bodies to become efficient metabolising mechanisms. This can be achieved through exercise.

Stand and deliver

As with most things in life, balance is the key and understanding what exercise is can help with creating this. For instance, you may move about quite a lot in your role. Many teachers stand when they teach and deliver their lessons with lots of bodily movement. Whilst most do not run around the room frantically, they are active to an extent. This is physical activity and it is important for your health as it encourages an active body – one that is more efficient at calorific expenditure – particularly when compared to the sedentary lifestyle of sitting in front of a computer all day. However, it may not be classed as exercise.

Exercise is defined as 'essentially a subcategory of physical activity' (Mikkelsen et al., 2017, p. 49) and it is often a planned activity, such as running or cycling. Generally, aerobic exercise raises the heart rate whilst anaerobic involves power or strength, although there is much variance in how these two forms play out. Anaerobic exercise will, of course, raise the heart rate to an extent and can make us out of breath; therefore, the two are perhaps more accurately conceptualised as being on a spectrum, where one morphs into the other. An example of this could be the Atlas stone event in a World's Strongest Man/Woman competition. Lifting it would be considered an anaerobic activity whilst running with it may move the athlete into aerobic activity. This can be complex, however, because sprinting is anaerobic (which is why the spectrum helps), but as a working distinction it is useful to think of anaerobic as requiring short bursts of energy and aerobic as relying on sustained movement where greater oxygen is needed.

Exercise

In recent years, there has been a wide range of studies that have noted the potential for exercise to have a positive effect on mental health (e.g. Abd El-Kader & Al-Jiffri, 2016; Anderson & Shivakumar, 2013; Apostolopoulos et al., 2014; DeBoer et al., 2012). According to Mikkelsen et al. (2017, p. 48), 'exercise can bring about many physiological changes which result in an improvement in mood state, self-esteem and lower stress and anxiety levels,' and this seems to be the case regardless of whether this exercise is aerobic – running, skipping and so on – or anaerobic, such as lifting heavy weights.

When we exercise, endorphins are produced in the brain (Harber & Sutton, 1984; Tendzegolskis et al., 1991). These have an analgesic effect and thus act as natural tranquilisers, relaxing us and alleviating stress and tension (Mikkelsen et al., 2017). Endorphins are thus seen as pleasure-inducing chemicals and help us to put a positive spin on things. This is not to say that we use exercise to ignore the reality of life; rather, the relaxing of our mental state helps us to resharpen our focus, to regain our composure, and to rethink our strategic defence. It allows us to be less immersed in our worries and concerns in order to generate a little objectivity, wherein we can put things into perspective. Physical exercise, then, can alleviate some mental health concerns and research has led some to suggest that it 'may be a viable adjunctive treatment for psychotherapy' (Mikkelsen et al., 2017, p. 49). However, this is not a blanket treatment and care should be taken to ensure that you have a balance of activities in your life. For instance, the findings for the effect of endorphins on anxiety is said to be mixed (DeBoer et al., 2012).

Fitting it in

It is often difficult to find the time to exercise when we lead such hectic lifestyles. In teaching in the FE sector, there is little space in the working week for taking on extra activities. On top of your planning, marking, and pastoral care, and a general inability to switch off thanks to the technology of the modern world (see Chapter 6), you now have the added task of going to the gym on the way home. However, there are ways of 'exercising' a little expedience within your workload in order to facilitate this. Firstly, there are still 24 hours in the day, and around 9 or 10 of those are likely to be needed for your evening's relaxation and sleep. If you do not get home until 7pm but need to eat, prepare for the next day, and engage in some housework before getting to bed by around 9pm (in order to get your full eight hours and rise at 6am for when the cycle continues), it is likely that you will need to examine how effective your day really is. This is an unusually long day, albeit typical for many teachers, and is unsustainable in the long run. Therefore, you may need to re-examine your stressors and identify a more realistic workload. For those who feel they can't, however, you may well ask the question, 'where is the time expected to come from to fit in exercising?'

In 2015, a study by Sjaan Gomersall and colleagues asked that question and recruited 129 participants to engage in either one of two prescribed exercise regimes or in a control group. From their study, Gomersall et al. (2015, p. 44) pointed out that taking on additional exercise requires a reduction in 'the time spent in other domains, such as sleep or screen time.' This appears obvious at first, yet it is surprising how much time is wasted during an average person's day that could be put to better use. Implementing an exercise regime, then, may mean that you have to reconfigure your day's events. However, there are ways to do this that involve fewer sacrifices of your important time. With a little negotiation, your busy schedule might start to reveal some accommodating opportunities.

A two-hour commute each day does little for the 68 assignments you have to mark by the end of the week (unless you can use your laptop on the train), but it can stimulate your thinking. And within this journey, there may also be time that you could be getting some exercise – power-walking to the train station, for instance, or getting off a stop early occasionally to fit in that extra hike. If you spend a great deal of time driving to work this can add extra constraints, and it is obviously time that cannot be used for exercise or marking. However, like travelling on a train, it can provide useful thinking time, and reflection is a powerful tool for dealing with difficulties and for developing resilience (reflection is addressed in more detail in Chapter 9).

Alternatively, you may choose to park a little further way to get those steps in. You might also consider utilising ten minutes of your lunch break, although it is likely you will need this valuable down time to balance your otherwise stressful day. However, if you are skipping lunch to plan a lesson or dealing with something that could possibly wait, it is likely that your stressors are overwhelming you. There are unexpected deadlines to meet at times, but you also need to ask yourself how efficient that last half hour was. When we are stressed, we often become less productive, wasting precious time on trying to focus and getting distracted with the things that we are not doing as our to-do list grows ever bigger. This is not a good strategy but quite difficult to avoid when you are tired and overwhelmed. This is one reason why balance is essential.

How you find the time for exercise, then, is something that you are likely to need to consider seriously. And if something has to yield to accommodate that exercise, how do you decide what that is? These are important considerations that need thinking through, the outcome of which can impact positively or negatively on your health. It will probably also determine how productive you are in your role. It may not merely be a task of moving your activities around but require strategic planning. For example, whilst reducing sedentary activities such as sitting and watching TV can be productive per se, cutting time from other areas of your day can present a challenge. It may also be that watching TV is the only valuable downtime you get and it enables you to switch off. It is necessary, then, to reflect on your decisions and to perhaps trial changes rather than implement them unwaveringly.

If you get out of bed at 6am to beat the rush hour traffic or need to arrive early due to restricted parking at the college, you can utilise this extra time. Perhaps it becomes soaked up with coffee and chats that are mostly unproductive. Healthy working relationships are important, but they can be developed in a more-structured manner. Your morning sessions can also give way to something more productive. This is what Gomersall et al. (2015, p. 44) term the 'isotemporal displacement of other activities.' If you find yourself 'killing time' in the morning just because you needed to get in early for that parking spot, yet stressed later on in the day because time is apparently not on your side, you should evaluate your situation. This is time that could be spent both on reducing your workload or on developing your physical health and fitness. You could decide to park further away than usual, for instance (perhaps a Smartwatch that counts your steps will motivate you), or you could arrange to go off for a stroll with some colleagues so that you can continue those important conversations and develop your working relationships at the same time.

In another way, exercise is not something that you need to incorporate every day. If you structure it well it will be easier to follow. If Monday, Wednesday and Friday are the mornings you have a routine of walking around the college for 20 minutes, that leaves your Tuesday and Thursday free for coffee and catch-ups. A small sacrifice, perhaps, but one which can have many positive benefits for your health. In this way, you retain a very similar lifestyle to the one you already had but make minor changes where there is scope to accommodate them. Moreover, your interactions with your colleagues are likely to be more meaningful now that they are structured in this way.

In addition to fitting in exercise in your working week, there is also the weekend. As mentioned, downtime is important and this is likely to be when you get most of this, but a small amount of exercise – just 30 minutes on either Saturday or Sunday (or both if you are feeling adventurous) can transform how you feel and how you cope with your workload once you get back to work on Monday morning. What is important, then, is having a balance of activities and there are many other ways in which you can create this balance. For instance, if your screen time is a concern, or is engulfing your evening, then reducing it by a small amount, such as 30 minutes, can be rewarding. Watching television is one of the most common pastimes that can be reduced to accommodate other activities (Robinson & Godbey, 1997). Whilst it can be a useful mechanism for shutting out the day's events and de-stressing through periods of inactivity – 'chewing gum for the eyes' (Peyre, 1944, p. 291) – it is a sedentary activity. And when combined with a full day of sitting at a desk on a non-teaching day, it can impact directly on our physical health and indirectly on our mental health. Television watching, then, may be the 'reservoir' of time that we can draw on to accommodate alternative activities (Gomersall et al., 2015). That half-hour walk outdoors will freshen you up and will allow you to refocus as you consciously choose to put your electronic addiction aside for a short time in order to reflect on your day.

Smartphones are amazing and transform our working lives in many ways, but part of their exceptional intelligence and ability to interact with our day-to-day functioning is their capacity to record exactly how much screen time we engage with daily. You can use this to your advantage by setting goals for reducing this time. If you have a Smartphone, it is likely you have often asked yourself questions such as 'where did those three hours go?' This is easily achieved, however, especially if you need to keep providing updates for your Twitter followers. Social media is highly time-consuming and may be an area you can reassess when you explore the balance of work and exercise. Reducing this time is a personal judgement call because it is likely to be an important aspect of your life, as well as a useful tool for widening your network. But the percentage of its contribution to your career could be gauged in order to limit your engagement with it. You can also keep up to date with your social media presence whilst in your rest periods in the gym.

Moreover, if you are research active, or even if you are merely keen to spread the word about your knowledge or experience of teaching, it is common to engage with social media in many ways. The pressure for FE teachers to engage in research is perhaps well intentioned but incredibly onerous as it often adds to a workload rather than replacing something. This leaves you in a difficult position and many accept that working through the evening and over weekends is part and parcel of their role. But the impact on your health is important and you will need to keep abreast of this.

Our bodies need downtime every day, and our minds need to go on standby too. That is one reason for sleeping, of course, but overload in the day will impact on that too. At the very least, a change of focus throughout the day can have a positive effect on your mental state. As Mikkelsen et al. (2017, p. 49) state, 'just 20–40 min of aerobic exercise can improve anxiety and mood for several hours.' Exercise will also improve the quality of sleep that you get.

The cyclical effect

When we are inundated, and time is constrained, this can impact on how much exercise we can engage in and we might devalue exercise as we prioritise our workload. This can impact on our mood and general positivity, and it has a cyclical effect because we then attempt to put in even more time and energy into reducing our workload. However, the more we feel apathetic and unmotivated and thus avoid exercise, the easier it becomes to rationalise our decision. Consequently, we feel the pressure of our workload more significantly as there is no outlet and feel further compelled to address it. This can result in prioritising it above many other things, such as healthy eating, as we grab that takeaway on the way home, and sleep – staying up late to catch up on work is common in teaching. Ironically, our productivity drops because we are tired, stressed, and temporarily undernourished, while the workload usually remains the same. Thus, the cycle continues. We are also less likely to engage in physical activity when we are feeling depressed due to lack of motivation (Wegner et al., 2014), and this is part of the cyclical effect because exercise could in fact alleviate those concerns.

Overdoing it: The exercise drug

The cyclical effect can also lead to overdoing it at times, particularly if you exercise to counter stress. Whilst exercise promotes good health and a positive outlook, there is a real danger in overexercising, the effects of which are extremely detrimental to both your physical and mental health (Mikkelsen et al., 2017). When combined with existing stress, excessive exercising can further overload you to the point of physical exhaustion and even mental breakdown, particularly if you identify your inability to sustain this lifestyle as a failure on your behalf (back to the cyclical effect). Moreover, overexercising does not always lead to changes in other behaviours. Gomersall et al. (2015, p. 46), for instance, found that 'imposed exercise loads were not compensated by reductions in physical activity or energy expenditure in other domains.' For this reason, a holistic approach is recommended, wherein you factor in as many of the important contributors of good health that you can – diet, sleep (and other forms of recuperation), exercise, routine, a balanced workload, and family time where possible.

Teaching can be a stressful career choice and arriving home after your teaching day with the feeling that you have been working out for hours – aching in your legs and a general feeling of fatigue – is a common occurrence. This can also impact on whether you choose to exercise as you will likely feel that you do not have enough energy left to go to the gym. But a short work-out is arguably worth striving for when you consider the benefit of switching off from work mode and the pleasurable rewards from the endorphin release that will help you to relax more in the evening. This is the point at which you need to consider the importance of balance. Too much exercise can impact on you physically, with symptoms such as dehydration, diarrhoea and headaches being common. People engage in too much exercise because it can be addictive, leading to dependence (Antunes et al., 2016). Exercise produces results so it is easy to slip into the misconception that more is better. Like most things in life, a balance is essential.

Exercise can be addictive and getting into the spirit of it and embracing it as a necessary feature of your life can be transformative. However, there are many detrimental effects from overindulgence that will impact on both your mind and your body in the opposite way in which you had hoped for. Overexercising can provide more stress to your life and it can wear you down physically. Becoming addicted to exercise can also result in the neglection of other areas of your life. And whilst you may feel empowered by your newfound fitness and/or physique and improved attitude, balance remains as important as ever. If your anxiety is related to workload, for instance, it will not be helpful to merely replace this workload with an excessive commitment to getting in the gym at all costs. Without a balance, some area in your life will suffer and the added pressure of feeling the need to exercise in times when it is either not possible or could jeopardise your teaching role is more stress-inducing than stress-relieving. In a recent study by Antunes et al. (2016, p. 187), it was found that for exercise-addicted athletes, 'exercise withdrawal results in an increase of depressive mood symptoms, fatigue, confusion, and anger and a loss of vigor.'

To do or not to do

Notwithstanding the above, exercise is, on the whole, beneficial for your healthy lifestyle. It should be structured into your routine to complement your career because its pros outweigh its cons. Exercise can reduce anxiety (DeBoer et al., 2012) whilst inactivity has been proven to perpetuate it (Mikkelsen et al., 2017). It is therefore a key ingredient in developing your resilience. You may be surprised at how engaging in 20–30 minutes of exercise actually makes you feel after a hard day's teaching and if done in moderation it will give you more energy.

Irregular hours

Studies on shift work and sleeping patterns often aim to capture the long-term health effects of such activities through a focus on sleep irregularity and the misalignment of our circadian rhythms (see Chapter 3). For instance, James et al. (2017) note that during periods of circadian misalignment – where our biological clock is dysregulated and our sleep patterns are disrupted or reformatted in a seemingly random manner – we may suffer from a hormonal balance and impairments in how we metabolise glucose. As such, we can feel hungry when we shouldn't and lose our appetite at key points in the day when our nutritional needs are at their highest. This can lead to difficulties with the regulation of bodyweight and may bring on obesity or other weight-related disorders. It is also stress-inducing and any biological changes that occur will likely be as a reaction to the upset in the regular functioning of the body.

Whilst teaching may not fall strictly into this category, the effect of working longer days and allowing our working lives to continue into our leisure time is hugely problematic. The overworked body often functions as if it is working through regular double shifts, and this will inevitably take its toll. Apart from the loss of time, we can also see the sacrifices that have to be made on other areas of our lives, such as diet and exercise, and this is counterproductive because attention to these areas can directly reduce our stress levels.

Routine and the importance of regulation

Humans love routine. It is not just that we can organise ourselves better, it is a biological necessity for a productive and healthy lifestyle. We crave routine because the body likes to be prepared for events and a routine helps your brain and body to function effectively. Indeed, research has shown that 'individuals in good health engage in highly routine health behaviors' (Arlinghaus & Johnston, 2019, p.142). Having a poor routine is confusing for both your mind and your body. Your brain will desperately try to make sense of the day's events and your body will need to regulate your biochemistry. A pattern is thus effective and beneficial. Your biological clock will not be too forgiving if you continually subject it to changes and upsets that jeopardise its potential for stability. Even at the weekend you should look to maintain some recognisable pattern to avoid unnecessary disruption.

Structured day hypothesis

The structured day hypothesis was proposed by Brazendale et al. (2017) and suggests that having a structured routine helps individuals to regulate their behaviours to form a pattern for exercise and diet. Studies have shown that the academic year is important for children as it provides a structured timetable with which they can engage and thus helps them to regulate their bodyweight (Brazendale et al., 2017; Moreno et al., 2019). In this way, children are able to work to deadlines and to conform to a structure, whilst holiday periods and weekends can be used for guilt-free relaxation (delayed gratification).

Structure, then, is an effective mechanism for taking control of your day, and it helps you avoid the unnecessary thinking that spontaneously structuring your day as you go can bring. Without a structure you are adding to your stress load. At the very least, you are providing your brain with more things to think about, and stress is often the build-up of lots of continuous thoughts, particularly where those thoughts involve grappling with an ongoing issue. A structured day can factor in time to address concerns and this enables you to shut them out of your head temporarily. This also includes your exercise regime. If you cycle to work, for instance, you may be able to discard thoughts of getting exercise each day because it is a part of your routine. However, if your exercise varies – you go the gym some nights, you swim whenever you can and so on, and this is not established as a routine, then you are giving yourself more to think about each day. Fortunately, even varied activities each day can still form a pattern if this can be replicated each week.

When you are thinking about how you can redress the balance of time spent during your day, then, and the potential for 'isotemporal displacement' (Gomersall et al. (2015, p. 44), you may want to look at the bigger picture in relation to your health. As seen, this can be done with relatively small changes that hardly impact on your daily routine.

Listening to your body

Your breathing is (obviously) important to you but for the most part we are unaware of it, it's just something we do automatically. But your breathing, and your heart rate, can tell you a lot about your health. If your heart rate is high, you may have high blood pressure and this could be related to a lack of exercise, albeit there are many other reasons. Stress will raise your heart rate and it is important to be aware of the wide variety of factors that will cause this stress. We associate stress with overwork but something as seemingly small as not getting enough sleep can also be a stressor (see Chapter 3). Alternatively, your blood pressure may be low and this is equally alarming. (Whether it is high or low you should consult your doctor.) Your breathing and heart rate, then, are indicators of your health and you should take care to monitor them. It may sound cliched but the expert of ourselves is usually ourselves. However, you have to become attuned to listening to what your body is telling you. Work pressures are often difficult to ignore but they can result in stress-related illnesses.

Dinners for winners: Fuelling your way to success

You may have heard of the old adage, 'you are what you eat.' The origin of this has been attributed to Jean Anthelme Brillat-Savarin who, in 1826, said, '*Dis-moi ce que tu manges, Je te dirai ce que tu es*' (*Tell me what you eat, I will tell you what you are*) (Brillat-Savarin, 1838, p. 14). Whilst this should not be taken literally, it does highlight the degree to which the food you consume supports/

constrains your development. Food is our fuel and thus an essential ingredient for developing and sustaining optimal health. But diet is often overlooked in the modern world. When we feel tired, unmotivated and believe we are struggling to cope with life, our resilience is low. This often results from a combination of factors, such as poor diet, a lack of exercise, irregular sleeping patterns, and an excessive workload. Of course, there are many factors in diagnosing why we feel low and apathetic at times, and each can be as important as the next, but diet is typically overlooked.

A healthy lifestyle is not just centred on going the gym. Diet, sleep and exercise are an important trilogy, but outlook often holds these together. Without a positive outlook, it is easy to neglect any (or all) of these areas. Moreover, the process is cyclical in that success in each will improve your outlook. With a poor perspective and inconsistent approach, you may find it difficult to address your concerns, to reduce your stressors, or be able to deal with situations as they arise. Resilience is dependent on different types of strength and it is at its best when our health is at an optimum level because other stressors can be minimised. Your outlook, therefore, should support your health and thus perpetuate the development of your resilience.

Mitigating stress

The evidence that stress can be mitigated through diet is unfortunately limited (Shively et al., 2020), although we do know that stress can deplete essential compounds that help us to fight it, such as Vitamin C and those in the B complex family. Some studies conducted with animals have suggested that diet can play a role in alleviating stress. Carol Shively and colleagues, for instance, looked at the effect of stress on a group of non-human primates (cynomolgus macaques). The study explored whether a Mediterranean diet would differ from a Western diet as some studies have shown that eating fruit and vegetables can have an impact on how stress is perceived (Nguyen et al., 2017). It was found that 'those fed the Mediterranean diet exhibited enhanced stress resilience as indicated by lower sympathetic activity, brisker and more overt heart rate responses to acute stress, more rapid recovery, and lower cortisol responses to acute psychological stress' (Shively et al., 2020, p. 1). It seems likely, then, that diet plays a key role in how stress affects us, and this should be combined with a structured routine that comprises a healthy balance of work and rest. Moreover, even if more research on this shows that diet has a neutral effect on stress, there is everything to gain from living that healthy lifestyle.

The Mediterranean diet has proven, through many studies, to be far superior to Western eating habits for both health and longevity (Mitrou et al., 2007; Sofi et al., 2013). Indeed, Lustig et al. (2012, p. 27) point out that 'Every country that has adopted the Western diet — one dominated by low-cost, highly processed food — has witnessed rising rates of obesity and related diseases.' The Mediterranean diet, however, is focused on providing your body with the necessary nutrition it needs to ward off threats such as illnesses, rather than the many unnatural ingredients that are often consumed in the West that tax our digestive systems. But is this enough in itself to prompt us into making those healthy choices? Some people will make sacrifices to ensure that their cars only function with premium fuel (regarded as efficient but usually the most expensive) yet fail to adopt a similar approach to their own bodies. Your diet is important, however, and it can make a significant contribution towards how you stave off (or deal with) stress and anxiety as you develop your resilience. Whilst there is not enough space here to outline the various food groups and their impact on the body – indeed, even to state what a healthy diet is exactly would do an injustice to the many books that have been written on the subject – it is useful to look at some basic aspects of food and nutrition so that we can begin to think about how our lifestyles can contribute to our poor resilience.

Food types

Our physical health is dependent on diet because it is food that drives us (energy), and it is food that helps us to recuperate. There are three main types of nutrients (albeit these can be broken down into many constituent parts): carbohydrates, proteins and fats (Michigan Medicine, 2021). These are essential for life and each one can be utilised as energy. However, some are more efficient at doing this than others and this helps to attribute different roles for each. Protein, for instance, is much more efficient when used to repair muscle rather than relying on it as a source of energy. Carbohydrates are known as the preferred source of energy as these are quick and easy to use and can be categorised as either complex (starch) or simple (sugar). Ideally, complex carbohydrates should be consumed as these are released slowly and thus provide sustained energy over longer periods. This is often essential when we are busy and there are potentially many hours in between meals. It is also a healthier choice as the body can deal with these carbohydrates more efficiently, avoiding the yo-yo effect on the blood sugar that can happen if only simple carbohydrates are consumed. Most of us will be familiar with this from reaching for that chocolate bar as a quick fix, only to have experienced a drop in energy levels after the effect has worn off.

Sugar

For many years the enemy of health has been fat (and to some extent it still plays a part). However, sugar, particularly the refined kind, is a major contributor to poor health, inactivity and even morbidity. Conditions such as diabetes, heart disease, stroke, and even certain forms of cancer have all been linked to high intakes of sugar and, more specifically, a generally poor diet. Excessive sugar consumption has also been linked to cognitive decline (Rippe & Angelopoulos, 2016). Of course, these factors often work in conjunction with other poor behaviours, but it is not uncommon for highly stressed individuals to suffer sleep deprivation, partake in very little exercise, and neglect their diet at the same time. Indeed, as these often go hand in hand they are usually determined by outlook. But why is sugar so attractive for many people? Like substance abuse, sugar has addictive qualities and can alter the brain's neuronal activity and emotional processing, thus creating 'pathophysiological consequences' (Jacques et al., 2019, p. 178). Moreover, Mosley (2017) argues that gut bacteria develop in response to what we eat. Thus, eating foods high in refined sugar causes a craving in this respect too as the appropriate gut bacteria grow and then need pacifying.

To counter this, you will need to encourage the growth of 'good' gut bacteria – that which utilises the healthy foods you eat – to support you. Gut bacteria are also essential because they can influence brain activity. Pinilla (2008, p. 568), for instance, points out that 'gut hormones that can enter the brain, or that are produced in the brain itself, influence cognitive ability.' Gut hormones are necessary for metabolism and thus for digesting and assimilating nutrients from our food. In this way, a healthy diet complements a healthy interior system. Poor dietary choices, then, can impact on your mood and it is difficult to find that inner resilience when you are tired and demotivated.

Overview

This chapter has briefly examined the contribution that good physical health can have on our resilience. It has outlined the importance of diet and exercise and a healthy, balanced routine. Building on the previous chapter, the necessity for ensuring a productive sleep pattern is also alluded to. However, this chapter is a mere introduction to these areas as they are broad and require much further exploration than is allowed here. It is recommended, then, that you use this chapter as a springboard for further investigation into how these factors can affect your working lifestyle and thus utilise the information in a bespoke manner. In order to address the stressors you face, it is advisable to identify what they are and then to devise a strategy for dealing with each. In the next chapters, we will look at a variety of such strategies that you can adopt to help you develop your resilience as you thrive in your teaching career.

Note

1 Always consult your doctor before exercising

References

Abd El-Kader, S.M. & Al-Jiffri, O.H. (2016). Aerobic exercise improves quality of life, psychological well-being and systemic inflammation in subjects with Alzheimer's disease. *African Health Sciences*, 16(4), 1045–1055.

Anderson, E. & Shivakumar, G. (2013). Effects of exercise and physical activity on anxiety. *Frontiers in Psychiatry*, 4(27). https://doi.org/10.3389/fpsyt.2013.00027

Antunes, H.K., Leite, G.S.F., Lee, K.S., Barreto, A.T., Santos, R.V.T., Souza, H.de Sá, Tufik, S. & Mello, M.T.de. (2016). Exercise deprivation increases negative mood in exercise-addicted subjects and modifies their biochemical markers. *Physiology & Behavior*, 156, 182–190.

Apostolopoulos, V., Borkoles, E., Polman, R. & Stojanovska, L. (2014). Physical and immunological aspects of exercise in chronic diseases. *Immunotherapy*, 6(10), 1145–1157.

Arlinghaus, K.R. & Johnston, C.A. (2019). The importance of creating habits and routine. *American Journal of Lifestyle Medicine*, 13(2), 142–144.

Brazendale, K., Beets, M.W., Weaver, R.G., Pate, R.R., Turner-McGrievy, G.M., Kaczynski, A.T., Chandler, J.L., Bohnert, A. & von Hippel, P.T. (2017). Understanding differences between summer vs. school obesogenic behaviors of children: The structured days hypothesis. *International Journal of Behavioral Nutrition and Physical Activity*, 14(100), 1–14. doi:10.1186/s12966–12017–0555–0552

Brillat-Savarin, J.A. (1838). *Physiologie du gout: Ou Méditations de gastronomie transcendante* [*The physiology of taste: Or meditations on transcendental gastronomy*]. 5th edn. Just Tessier, Libraire.

DeBoer, L.B., Powers, M.B., Utschig, A.C., Otto, M.W. & Smits, J.A.J. (2012). Exploring exercise as an avenue for the treatment of anxiety disorders. *Expert Review of Neurotherapeutics*, 12(8), 1011–1022. doi:10.1586/ern.12.73

Gomersall, S.R., Nortonc, K., Maher, C., English, C. & Olds, T.S. (2015). In search of lost time: When people undertake a new exercise program, where does the time come from? A randomized controlled trial. *Journal of Science and Medicine in Sport*, 18, 43–48.

Harber, V.J. & Sutton, J.R. (1984). Endorphins and exercise. *Sports Medicine*, 1(2), 154–171.

Jacques, A., Chaaya, N., Beecher, K., Ali, S.A., Belmer, A. & Bartlett, S. (2019). The impact of sugar consumption on stress driven, emotional and addictive behaviors. *Neuroscience & Biobehavioral Reviews*, 103, 178–199. https://doi.org/10.1016/j.neu biorev.2019.05.021

James, S.M., Honn, K.A., Gaddameedhi, S. & Van Dongen, H.P.A (2017). Shift work: Disrupted circadian rhythms and sleep – implications for health and well-being. *Current Sleep Medicine Reports*, 3, 104–112. doi:10.1007/s40675–40017–0071–0076

Lustig, R., Schmidt, L. & Brindis, C. (2012). The toxic truth about sugar. *Nature*, 482, 27–29. https://doi.org/10.1038/482027a

Michigan Medicine (2021). *Carbohydrates, proteins, fats, and blood sugar*. University of Michigan Health. https://www.uofmhealth.org/health-library/uq1238abc#:~: text=Carbohydrates%20are%20used%20for%20energy,%2C%20muscle%2C%20and %20other%20proteins.&text=Broken%20down%20into%20glucose%2C%20used% 20to%20supply%20energy%20to%20cells

Mikkelsen, K., Stojanovska, L., Polenakovic, M., Bosevski, M. & Apostolopoulos, V. (2017). Exercise and mental health. *Maturitas*, 106, 48–56.

Mitrou, P.N., Kipnis, V., Thiébaut, A.C., Reedy, J., Subar, A.F., Wirfält, E., Flood, A., Mouw, T., Hollenbeck, A.R., Leitzmann, M.F. & Schatzkin, A. (2007). Mediterranean dietary pattern and prediction of all-cause mortality in a US population: Results from the NIH-AARP Diet and Health Study. *Archives of Internal Medicine*, 167(22), 2461–2468. doi:10.1001/archinte.167.22.2461

Moreno, J.P., Crowley, S.J., Alfano, C.A., Hannay, K.M., Thompson, D. & Baranowski, T. (2019). Potential circadian and circannual rhythm contributions to the obesity epidemic in elementary school age children. *International Journal of Behavioral Nutrition and Physical Activity*, 16(25), 1–10. doi:10.1186/s12966–12019–0784–0787

Mosley, M. (2017). *The clever guts diet: How to revolutionise your body from the inside out.* London: Short Books Ltd.

Nguyen, B., Ding, D. & Mihrshahi, S. (2017). Fruit and vegetable consumption and psychological distress: Cross-sectional and longitudinal analyses based on a large Australian sample. *British Medical Journal Open*, 7(3), 1–9.

Peyre, H. (1944). *Writers & their critics: A study of misunderstanding.* Ithaca, NY: Cornell University Press.

Pinilla, F.G. (2008). Brain foods: The effects of nutrients on brain function. *Nature Reviews. Neuroscience*, 9(7), 568–578. doi:10.1038/nrn2421

Rippe, J.M. & Angelopoulos, T.J. (2016). Relationship between added sugars consumption and chronic disease risk factors: Current understanding. *Nutrients*, 8(11), 1–19. doi:10.3390/nu8110697

Robinson, J.P. & Godbey, G. (1997). *Time for life: The surprising ways Americans use their time.* University Park, PA: The Pennsylvania State University Press.

Shively, C.A., Appt, S.E., Chen, H., Day, S.M., Frye, B.M., Shaltout, H.A., Silverstein-Metzler, M.G., Snyder-Mackler, N., Uberseder, B., Vitolins, M.Z. & Register, T.C. (2020). Mediterranean diet, stress resilience, and aging in nonhuman primates. *Neurobiology of Stress*, 13, 1–10. https://doi.org/10.1016/j.ynstr.2020.100254

Sofi, F., Macchi, C., Abbate, R., Gensini, G.F. & Casini, A. (2013). Mediterranean diet and health status: An updated meta-analysis and a proposal for a literature-based adherence score. *Public Health Nutrition*, 17(12), 2769–2782. doi:10.1017/S1368980013003169

Tendzegolskis, Z., Viru, A. & Orlova, E. (1991). Exercise-induced changes of endorphin contents in hypothalamus: Hypophysis, adrenals and blood plasma. *International Journal of Sports Medicine*, 12(5), 495–497.

Wegner, M., Helmich, I., Machado, S., Nardi, A.E., Arias-Carrion, O. & Budde, H. (2014). Effects of exercise on anxiety and depression disorders: Review of meta-analyses and neurobiological mechanisms. *CNS & Neurological Disorders – Drug Targets*, 13 (6), 1002–1014. doi:10.2174/1871527313666140612102841

Part 2

Strategising for resilience

5 You and your approach

Getting to know yourself

Developing resilience is often linked to confidence, self-esteem and aspirations as it is about personal and professional growth. The more you excel in these areas, the more likely you will be able to strengthen your ability to endure a difficult situation. Successful development of these characteristics is often dependent on the degree of self-awareness you hold, and setbacks can be overcome more effectively as you learn to identify your strengths and weaknesses. Knowing your strengths will help you to fully utilise those aspects of your character that will bring success. For instance, if you know that you are good at dealing with other people's problems, you might want to use this as a strategy for distancing yourself from your own difficulties. Imagine it is your friend who has the problem: What advice would you give?

Your weaknesses, on the other hand, will prevent you from overcoming problems and will challenge your resilience. These must be identified so that you can plan accordingly. To exemplify this point, let us suppose you like to deal with your difficulties alone. Whilst talking to others is useful to establish perspective, you know this is not an option for you. However, you could decide to keep a diary of your thoughts and attempt to link these thoughts together across the week. This will help you to glean an overview of your thought processes and you may be able to evaluate the journey a little more objectively. Because you are thinking about your situation in retrospect, as well as when you were immersed in it, you should be able to form a more rounded perspective of it. Donald Schön's writings on *reflection-in-action* and *reflection-on-action* can provide a framework for understanding this (see Chapter 9). Knowing yourself well, then, can enable you to outline a bespoke strategy for restoring stability in your life and career. This personalised approach can save you a lot of time and energy and will build your confidence, thereby contributing to the building of your resilience.

In order to return to your usual practice, particularly when you have faced a difficult situation or a traumatic event, you will need to know how well you are doing. This is dependent on how in touch you are with your emotions. Getting to know yourself is essential because you can then understand how you

DOI: 10.4324/9780367824211-7

can function more effectively by reading the signs. However, these can be misidentified. Weariness, for instance. Many people agree that their weariness arises from the stressful toll of working long hours yet fail to address their sleeping patterns and general health concerns (see Chapter 3). They then become frustrated and struggle to cope. It would be more productive, however, to identify an appropriate target for those frustrations so that you can delineate the difference between your individual capabilities and the expectations of the institution. For example, some people feel frustrated that they cannot cope and put pressure on themselves to perform better; but identifying what they can and cannot do – particularly in relation to situations that are beyond their control – could enable them to understand that frustration and thus be more in tune with their emotions.

When facing some of the many other emotionally driven instances that life throws at us, such as tragic illnesses, losing a loved one, going through a divorce, buying and selling a house, or losing a job, resilience is necessary because, although it does not take away the pain or resolve the problem, it does better equip us to deal with the situation. Finding a balance between what are usual, and often inevitable, challenges of life and those that are overwhelming and seemingly insurmountable is a crucial way forward. We are likely to need more resilience for high-pressured situations but we should hold on to the understanding that these are often temporary. However, our typical, everyday pressures can also be as impactful if we dismiss their potential and thus fail to deal with them appropriately.

Resilience can only help us deal with what we have the capacity to deal with, whilst poor planning or a lack of resilience can lead us to perceive all challenges as insurmountable. Conceptually, and arguably for clarity, we should distinguish between challenges that can be tackled and challenges that are too difficult to overcome. The terms 'hurdle' and 'barrier' are thus useful in helping to plan efficiently. Hurdles hinder progress whilst barriers prevent it. If we categorise something as a barrier, we know that we will be wasting our time in attempting to overcome it and will thus need to address this in another manner, such as through help from colleagues.

Conceptualising your approach: Hurdles and barriers

Hurdles are the challenges we must overcome and can be tangible – such as the physical constructions facing athletes who engage in hurdling – or abstract, as in the belief that we will personally find it difficult to do something because we do not feel we have the experience. Tangible hurdles are usually straightforward in that they can be seen, they can be gauged, and a plan of action can be formed that will be empirically tested. Abstract hurdles, however, are more complex; and whilst they feel real in the sense that they are holding us back, they can easily be misidentified. It is thus important to remember what the challenge is and to categorise it accordingly.

The more challenging items we face are barriers. These not only hinder our performance, they prevent us from achieving our goals. Barriers in this sense cannot be overcome and are thus impregnable. To circumnavigate this concern, we need to either find a way of reconceptualising a barrier as a hurdle, or of identifying its composite elements. This may seem like petty semantics, but the language we use represents how we perceive difficulties and thus determines how we approach them. Let's reify this with a simple example. You are trapped in a storeroom in your college. The latch on the door clicked by accident and the door closed, locking you inside. For all intents and purposes, the walls are barriers. They will prevent you from getting out so you look for the weak areas to see whether these could be redefined as hurdles. The wall with the door is solid but we know that the door itself is only being held by a small piece of metal known as a latch. This weakens the concept of the door as a barrier and recategorises it as a hurdle. If we find a way to push the latch back into its casing, the door will open. This particular wall can now be overcome, although it will not be is easy to open the door and may require a tool. Some may even decide that they cannot open the door at all and identify it as a barrier.

Perception, then, is important and we can see how different people have varied approaches to the same concern. This means that the problem is not so much a mathematical one, with only one answer, but a multi-layered challenge, where solutions depend on the person involved. A locksmith in the storeroom may free herself in seconds using her professional knowledge and skills, whilst a physically strong individual may bash the door down. Each has achieved their aim and utilised their particular strength. Of course, many may kick at the door several times yet achieve little more than swollen toes. What this scenario shows us is that how we gauge a situation is crucial for diagnosing a plan of defence/attack. Needlessly kicking the door might help to vent some anger and frustration but it won't necessarily open it. However, if another wall happened to have a window in it, this would be another potential hurdle.

If we learn to reconceptualise our problems, then, as hurdles or barriers, we become better equipped to deal with them. We can also resist yielding as we recognise that there is a way of overcoming this challenge, even if that way has yet to be identified. How we interpret a situation usually determines how confident we are at dealing with it, and categorising a challenge as a hurdle can be empowering. Moreover, knowing what we are dealing with can develop optimism, which is 'a key trait for resilient people' (Aguilar, 2018, p. 150). Fortunately, if we transpose the analogy into something more abstract, the same principle applies.

In our professional lives we often come across challenges and overcoming these can be more achievable if they are challenges we are familiar with. This is why the initial identification is so important. And yet, it is also easy to misdiagnose a problem as being bigger than it is or even perceiving it as insurmountable. Without that familiarity, we enter the unknown and speculate what we think the challenge is. And at this point, many give up. Even the locksmith in the storeroom might have reacted with anger and thumped the door before reflecting on the situation. This is the stage that some people find themselves in when a situation appears bleak. It is where some people give up whilst others rethink the situation.

> **Box 5.1 Exercise**
>
> As an English teacher, you have been working with a small group of students recently delivering English to a functional skills (FS) class. However, your line manager has informed you that from the following term you will also be teaching (FS) maths. Although you have an A level yourself, this was over fifteen years ago so you are not confident that you can deliver this. Using two columns, note down all the reasons why this could be a hurdle and then do the same with the barrier category. As you do so, try to be objective so that you can compare each list and assess the situation overall.

Accurately identifying our problems is essential as it is often when hurdles are perceived to be barriers that we give up. For instance, you have to finish some marking by the next morning but you really do not want to take the work home with you as you have friends coming to your house. This is causing you stress and anxiety as you dwell on the thought that it might not get done. Moreover, you have avowed to only take things home in emergency situations and you have already worked three evenings in the last week. This is now impacting on your health and you feel overwhelmed by the workload and frustrated with your work–home balance. First, you should categorise the challenge: in what way could this be a hurdle? Sometimes we allow pressures to enlarge and thus perceive them as more important than they actually are. You may have decided that this is insurmountable (barrier) because taking work home is part of your job. Alternatively, it may be that there are times to fit this in before you go home (hurdle).

There are two ways forward with this problem. One, you resist taking work home on the whole and look for ways to incorporate it into your day, perhaps requesting that your workload in other areas should be lightened. Two, the barrier can be broken down into individual hurdles. Each night you take work home would be a hurdle and you could refuse to do this some nights. Perhaps you originally accepted to take work home with you occasionally but this gesture has now been abused. You should resist the situation and maybe raise it with your line manager – gestures of goodwill need to be reciprocal. If you choose to accept the evening work, you should weigh up the impact; merely persevering is not always a healthy response. If you have identified a problem, it needs resolving in some way.

The point of recategorising something is to help you decide how you will tackle it. Is it too big for one person? Perhaps it is and that is why it seems insurmountable. But to what extent have you made it bigger than it is? Maybe you have even underestimated the work involved in completing this task. If so, you may need to recategorise it so that you have a realistic depiction of what is expected. This will help you to reduce any blame you attribute to yourself for not being able to complete it, and it will help you to present your case that it is overwhelming. Recategorising a task is important and should not be under-valued. Ask yourself whether you are being unreasonable or whether it is an unrealistic expectation. You can also speak to a work colleague and glean their advice as this will help to situate your perspective.

Habitual behaviour

Building new habits and challenging our existing, stagnant ones is essential for developing resilience. Habits are the behaviours we undertake regularly and they condition us into a routine wherein we are confident in what we are doing. Often, we do not have enough resilience because a problem challenges our familiarity and breaks our routine. It pushes us out of our comfort zone, and as creatures of regulation we do not always deal with this in the best way. This can affect resilience because our routine is a pattern in which we have normalised the way we operate. However, our regular way of performing might also be perpetuating the problem.

If you have poor resilience, you may need to break your cycle of thinking and behaving. For example, if you don't promote yourself in the staff room and around your institution in general, or have become complacent in your role even though you yearn to move up the ladder, then it is likely that you feel promotion is not for you. You may dream of having a managerial role in your institution because you have great ideas that could really transform the running of the department yet feel that you could not cope in a position of responsi-bility because you don't have experience in dealing with challenges. You believe that this is a realistic self-impression but it is possible that you feel this way because you have low self-esteem. This is a cyclical process and can impact on your resilience, whereupon you no longer feel equipped to cope with change and thus cling to your routine. But change is an inevitable aspect of life and acknowledging this, however difficult, is crucial if you want to thrive in the workplace.

Change happens regularly and it is incredibly difficult, sometimes, when that change moves us onto uncomfortable terrain. This can affect our stress levels because we are no longer confident in predicting outcomes. It is an extremely difficult type of change to deal with. An example of this would be an institu-tional restructure that presents a significant adaptation to your role. You may even be facing the possibility of your post being disestablished. This is a difficult position to be in because your negotiating powers are likely to have been dra-matically reduced, and it is unfortunately a common one. Recent austerity within the sector has resulted in many similar occurrences, such as the institu-tional mergers from 2015 and closures of numerous sites. This is difficult even for the most resilient among us. However, if we accept that most change pushes us out of our comfort zone then we can develop a little mechanistic resilience, wherein we try to remove as much emotional connection as possible. This is a temporary solution to coping with the change and is purely designed to get you through; the most effective way to deal with any change beyond our control, of course, is to embrace it, but that can be extremely difficult. And you should resist unreasonable change where possible.

Your resilience is often stronger when you can revert to habitual behaviour; thus, while new experiences are effective methods for learning, at some point you need to regulate these experiences so that you can draw on your reserves of resilience. New experiences can generate additional stressors so forming patterns in what you do will help to prevent this.

A realistic approach to identifying your needs

Arguably, the first step in identifying your stressors is to be as accurate as possible. We are often unaware of the demands on us and feel that we are coping well, and outlining what these demands are, and how they impact on us, can be daunting. Identifying a problem can reduce its potential damage because we have a more realistic perspective of the threat we face. It also develops our confidence as we feel in control of the situation. A realistic approach helps us to put our difficulty into perspective, then, and reduces its potency; it is often the fears that we cannot identify that magnify in our heads. For example, think about the strategies of a horror film. A person alone in a house who hears a noise is unprepared for that threat and this adds to the intensity of the fear. Is it a person? Is it a group of people? Are they armed? Is it a dangerous animal? Is it supernatural? This type of fear is based on novelty (Gray, 1987) and the person undergoing it may become stressed as they to deal with it. It may also produce anxiety because it is difficult to predict the outcome. Resilience in this situation could be drawn from prior experiences, however, perhaps identifying the noise as a potentially non-threatening source. However, this could also be a naïve approach which makes the fear a valuable emotion.

'Fear memory' is a key mechanism for survival (Devau, 2016) but in this situation we can only draw on similar experiences and hope that this prepares us. If the person in the house can account for the noise as the family cat having knocked over a vase the threat is discarded. Strangely, even if the attributed noise is an intruder, our perception of the potency of the threat may still be reduced once the intruder is identified, especially if we feel we can overcome him. Fear of the unknown, then, can exacerbate a threat and failing to accurately identify your stressors presents an unequal fight. This is a battle that is difficult to prepare for and can result in increased stress levels. If we recognise the extent of a problem, we can allocate the appropriate time and effort needed to tackle it and identify whether we could do this alone or need help. The unknown reduces our agency because we are unaware of whether it is in our capacity to deal with the situation. Table 5.1 highlights some of the differences in the potential impact of an identified problem versus an unknown one. For the purpose of this exercise, a problem would remain 'unknown' until the full extent of its impact could be understood.

Table 5.1 Problems and effects

An identified problem	An unknown problem
Can be measured.	The full extent of this is not known and can grow in our heads.
Time can be realistically allocated to deal with it.	The time needed to overcome this cannot be identified as we do not know the scale of the problem.
Resources needed are known and can be accrued – e.g. financial, human.	Opportunities may be missed and we are likely to be underprepared.
An appropriate plan of defence can be formed.	Forming a plan is difficult as it can only be generic and thus may be highly inappropriate. This can generate anxiety as we speculate the 'what if.'
An endpoint can be gauged.	Seems never-ending and may exacerbate stress levels.
Can develop confidence and help us to feel in control.	Increases fear and anxiety, reduces agency and confidence.

Box 5.2 Case study

Calvin was working late every night after college and most weekends. He had designed a website for teachers and had built a network of FE colleagues. He was in charge of overseeing the progress of this group and he regularly blogged about his teaching experiences. Calvin also felt pressured to maintain the readership he had amassed over the previous twelve months. His two small children loved being with him but would often only see him at the weekends as they would be in bed by the time he arrived home from work.

Calvin was supposed to be going with his family on a vacation during the Christmas period but he had cancelled due to work commitments. He would often go into the college during the half term to prepare for the coming weeks and to catch up with any outstanding marking. His family chose to continue with their Christmas vacation whilst Calvin stayed at home and caught up with his work. Without realising it, being away from his family was adding to his stress.

Calvin believed he was mentally and physically healthy, although he had ceased his former hobby of painting and was no longer training with the village's five-a-side football team. Between September and February, Calvin had grown increasingly weary and was at the point of exhaustion when the Covid-19 pandemic resulted in a UK lockdown. Calvin was now tasked with revising his teaching resources to cater for online teaching. He countered this tiredness with excessive amounts of coffee drinking and would boast to his colleagues how it was possible to get by on less than five hours' sleep per night. But Calvin was not recovering and was instead adding to his workload by developing resources for other courses and posting them on his website. He even took it upon himself to write short courses for teachers' professional development. Calvin's health began to falter but he continued regardless.

Because Calvin enjoyed what he did, he was oblivious to the effect it was having on him. He felt that he was resilient and strong enough to cope with a wide variety of interests, but the pressure caught up with him and he was advised by his doctor to step away from his commitments. For Calvin, it had been difficult to identify his stressors as he had attached a label of pleasure and reward to these stressors; as such, he was ill-prepared and his illness led to a breakdown where he was forced to take sick leave. Fortunately, Calvin used his rest period to reflect on his situation and eventually recovered. He returned to work with a reduced teaching load and reassessed his other commitments. Calvin now understands the cumulative effect of the stressors and has constructed a balanced approach. He finishes work at a set time every day (with some minor exceptions but these are monitored), he has encouraged his teacher colleagues to contribute to the blog and the website in general to spread the workload, and he spends more time with his family. In his own words, he stated, 'I didn't realise that I was actually stressed. I was constantly thinking about not seeing my wife and children but the impact didn't register with me. I felt guilty all the time but I didn't do anything about it. I think that was piling the stress on as well. By the end I was burnt out.'

Commentary

There are many important messages to learn from Calvin's situation in the case study, but I shall concentrate on just four key points. First, balance is critical in our lives. We are governed by biological needs and the necessity for routine. The number of hours we sleep, the amount we eat, the social interactions we need, and so on, all contribute to how healthy our outlook is (see Chapters 3 and 4). We can see from the case study that too much of anything – whether good or bad – can be detrimental to our health. However, it is often difficult to recognise when something perceived as good is actually harmful. Calvin's 'healthy' obsession with his love of teaching soon became unhealthy. Biologically, our bodies and our minds crave routine and stability (homeostasis), and this provides us with a much stronger stance in the game of survival. Maintenance is easier to implement when there is little disruption.

Second, stress is influential and can impinge on our lives in a variety of ways. Calvin's actions impacted on his family but the stress he was undergoing could be alleviated by disseminating aspects of his workload. This includes Calvin's self-imposed tasks, such as the maintenance of the website. Calvin was unaware of the impact this stress was having on his health because he was engaging in activities he enjoyed; but he also chose to ignore the effect this lifestyle was having on his loved ones.

Third, some stressors are explicit and clearly detrimental to our health. Others, however, are more pernicious, particularly if they align with pleasurable activities and thus can be difficult to identify. Calvin was aware that he was busy but seemed oblivious to the fact that he was in fact overloaded with work and the various activities he chose to undertake because his stress developed over time.

Fourth, a major concern for Calvin's lifestyle is that there was no potential leeway for meeting new challenges. That is, his commitments did not allow for extra pressures to be added; and in the case of Covid-19, these extra pressures were deemed to be essential working practices for teachers. Moving teaching online was necessary in order to continue to commit to the contracted teaching agreement from both the institutions and the staff. For most teachers, this was in addition to what they already did and was thus stressful. For Calvin, however, it prompted a breakdown as he was already near his maximum workload capacity prior to the Covid-19 outbreak. Calvin made a full recovery because he reflected deeply on his situation and re-learned how to take control of it. He also became much more aware of his potential stressors.

References

Aguilar, E. (2018). *Onward: Cultivating emotional resilience in educators*. London:Jossey-Bass.

Devau, G. (2016). Introduction to a biological basis of fear. *Gérontologie et société*, 38150 (2), 17–29.

Gray, J.A. (1987). *The psychology of fear and stress*. 2nd edn. Cambridge: Cambridge University Press.

6 Autonomy and control

Retaining control

In stressful situations, it is important that you acknowledge your responsibility as well as your limitations. This ensures you remain in control, even though there will be many areas that you cannot impact on, and that you can regulate the way you react to a situation. Stress is only the effect that we allow a situation to have on our mind and our body, and whilst this is easier said than done (it is difficult to ignore the rantings of your boss when you are in fear of losing your livelihood), it does mean that at least a vestige of control is yours. This can even earn you respect because not all seemingly unscrupulous managers are beyond change. Indeed, some are under so much pressure themselves they are not even aware that they are passing it on to you. Your boss may also be in need of resilience and it is possible that he/she is uncomfortable with the choices he/she has been given. There may even be unreasonable decisions that your boss is required to implement. If you do not voice your concerns, it can be difficult for your seemingly unscrupulous manager to empathise with your situation. After all, your lack of complaints is probably perceived as consent for your workload. Without making that connection, you also run the risk of resenting someone you work with, an act that can have far more detrimental effects on you than on the person involved (especially if they are unaware of it). This is unwanted, negative energy.

Many families who have lost loved ones to murderers eventually progress to a stage where they either forgive the murderer or become numb towards them, putting their hatred and urge for vengeance aside in an attempt to ditch their negative energy. This is obviously extremely difficult to do as it can feel like it is condoning the perpetrator's behaviour; but it has its merits in that it can reduce some of the stress the victims are suffering. Anger and resentment can eat away at us and those individuals who have moved on from such horrific situations (not, of course, forgetting their lost loved ones) have great strength of character, demonstrating amazingly high levels of resilience. This is a positive approach to an otherwise horrific event and it is used to avoid holding on to negative energy. It is unfair for a victim to continue suffering and many have learned that remaining angry merely perpetuates their suffering. Whilst grieving

DOI: 10.4324/9780367824211-8

is an important human condition that should not be denied, self-tortuous actions are often counterproductive.

What we can learn from this situation, then, is the incredible resilience shown by the people involved. It is not about taking a selfish approach, and it is not about merely saying 'why should I suffer?' because some of the suffering is contained within the grieving. It is about asking whether any of this torment is achieving anything, and whether there is an alternative that will bring something positive back. In this way, the person retains control and is even aware of their limitations.

Many of us have wanted to turn the clock back at times because of mistakes made or poor decisions taken, but expending energy into regret serves little in the way of resolution. Acknowledging limitations is an important strategy for letting go of the negative things we hold on to, and it frees us up to focus our energy on more productive ventures. We cannot change the past but we can change how it affects us. And we can draw on our experiences to cope with unexpected changes.

Focussing on something that is not within your power to change can be destructive as it consumes energy and is futile. It will also likely be counter-productive for your resilience as it is highlighting your constraints and engendering frustration. It is fine to have limitations but if changing something is not within your control then there may be other ways to find resolution.

Adapting to new circumstances

Building resilience in teaching may appear difficult because it is a profession that is often in flux. Changes occur regularly and staff may need to adapt quickly. This is, however, a positive aspect of teaching in relation to resilience as those who have dealt with many changes are usually more resilient and adept at adapting their practice.

Often, we feel we lack resilience but what we may be avoiding is a change in our circumstances. The more resilient we are, the better we deal with change; but we have to be comfortable with that change. Resilience can help us to achieve this and the more change we have in our lives the better we are, usually, at dealing with it. This is the knock-on effect of resilience and it is cyclical. Most of us do not like change; it even goes against our biological needs as the body needs regulation (homeostasis), and having a routine for diet, sleep and activity supports this (Davies, 2016). Change lifts us out of our comfort zones and can put us in what we feel is an invidious position. We are forced to deal with the unknown and this is unnerving and anxiety-inducing because we do not know for sure if we are prepared or if we are even capable. But entering the unknown is good sometimes and the more we do it, the more, ironically, it becomes familiar. We may not know what is expected of us but we can feel confident in predicting what is likely to occur.

Experiences can trigger implicit forms of resilience that we are not always conscious of. When we respond to change we learn from that experience. And having done this on numerous occasions we at least learn that the outcome is not always negative. The unknown becomes more predictable and this gives us comfort. We know from experience, therefore, that we have survived similar situations so we use this to grow our confidence. This is less of a conscious intention to survive and more of a subconscious strength. We may even become aware of our hidden resilience and this can spur us on. To draw on a useful metaphor: think about the proposition that a stranger is only someone you have never met and consider the thinking that everyone you know was once a stranger to you. If you do not have worries about meeting new people then that is because you have resilience in meeting people. You are experienced at it and you are confident that you will weather each encounter. In a similar way, change is something we can become confident in meeting once we have grown accustomed to it.

Emotional intelligence

Teaching can be an emotionally driven profession and your emotional intelligence influences how you will respond to a situation. Staying in touch with your emotions will help you to gauge how you connect with the situation. If you can identify the emotion that you are experiencing, you should ask yourself if it is contributing to your progress within that situation. Destructive emotions will need to be curbed and how well you do this is based on how you connect with the situation and your emotional intelligence. You should ask yourself what role your emotions are playing in this situation. Anger, for instance, might have a role in motivating us but is it really going to result in a positive outcome if it is poorly channelled? Your anger may be causing you to lose control, to shift blame to where it does not belong, and to say things that are not contributing to a resolution. Alternatively, you can utilise your emotions to benefit you. For example, sadness might seem like an unwanted emotion yet help you to feel empathy for someone.

Having strong emotional intelligence will help you to be more objective and to see the effect your actions are having. As you become more experienced in your role, particularly if you are teaching, your emotional intelligence will develop along with your interpersonal skills. Teachers usually become adept at connecting with others and thus can often empathise with other people's emotions. This is a useful skill as it means they are in control of their emotions and are aware of the subjectivity of their perspective.

Teaching is a profession where a passion for developing others is a major strength, and teachers are often committed to what they do because of their emotional connection with their role. But emotions are powerful, make-or-break aspects of your personality and you should utilise them wisely. Once you have finetuned your emotional intelligence you will be in a stronger position to develop your emotional resilience, your ability to adapt to stressful situations. Emotional intelligence, then, is about identifying, connecting with, and controlling (i.e. using to their full effect) the emotions you bring to a situation.

Such emotions are strong feelings and push you into a subjective appraisal of a situation. In many ways this is useful as it encourages you to draw on your experiences and to connect with the situation. But a challenging situation is likely to require approaches that you may not be in a position to take if you are emotionally immersed. You may need to create distance in order to think more objectively.

Begin by taking yourself out of the situation. If it is personal to you then you may need the advice of a colleague or your line manager. Second, try to see a situation from an alternative perspective. The reflective model advocated by Stephen Brookfield is useful here. He suggested that viewing a situation through other perspectives helps us to be more critical and thorough in our understanding of it. The four lenses Brookfield (1998) advocates are self, student, colleague, and literature (see Chapter 9). Viewing a situation in this way enables us to think more objectively.

Factoring in time

In the hectic working arrangements of the FE teacher, time is typically viewed as a luxury. We often know what we need to do yet struggle to find the time or space in which this can be achieved. To address this, we should take control of our time (see also Chapter 7 for how to manage your timetable). By allocating just five minutes per day to reflect on a problem, you are already on your way towards finding its solution. To ensure that you sustain this approach, you may need to use a timer. If you run over time, you are in danger of giving up. This is because an 'all or nothing' approach means taking on heavy demands and this commitment becomes easy to relinquish. Five minutes will allow you to resume working on your other commitments yet will satisfy you in that you have begun to address the problem rather than ignoring it. The time allocated is small but should leave you feeling guilt-free, providing you make the five minutes count. For instance, brainstorm your ideas onto paper (or computer) and don't concern yourself over the presentation of this, other than ensuring you can return to it without confusion. It is important to get your ideas onto the page, perhaps in the manner of a 'stream of consciousness,' and you can make sense of them the following day. Once your five minutes ends, stop what you are doing. This is necessary because if you do not stop, when you try the same exercise again the next day your brain will remember that you reneged on the deal and may try to talk you out of it.

Five minutes a day is not a long time, and you should build this up to ten and even 30 minutes if you are facing numerous challenges throughout the week. This small-step approach is useful because it means that you are not shutting the problem out but actively dealing with it (or at least addressing it in some manner). The short period also means you can continue with your day without worrying that this issue is detracting you from your work. The alternative to this is to leave it but this will likely have the opposite effect of what you are trying to achieve. Instead of your approach strengthening over time due to the cumulation of the five-minute periods spent addressing it, it may be that your problem is the one that is growing. This can also stimulate stress and anxiety because you are failing to deal with the problem, primarily by refusing to accept it. As Peterson (2019, p. 350) notes, 'The parts of your brain that generate anxiety are more interested in the fact that there is a plan than in the details of that plan.' Concerns often remain in our heads until we have either resolved them or we have put a plan in place to address them. As such, you are pacifying your mind in a way that alleviates the pressure to act.

Categorising your concerns

In order to achieve something we need to give it our full attention, or at least the majority of it. How many times have you driven home and not actually remembered the journey? 'How did I get home?' you wonder. 'I don't recall driving. I got in my car at the office and now I'm here. What happened in the meantime?' Of course, you did drive your car home, and you felt you must have been paying some attention, but you generally coursed along on 'autopilot.' When this happens we are functioning by using memory to guide our behaviour (Willingham, 2021). This is when we revert to habit, or that which over a hundred years ago was referred to as 'the proceeding of the mind in such a way that the familiar processes are in consciousness' (Andrews, 1903, p. 121). Another concept linking to this is automaticity, often seen as cognitive processing that appears to be undertaken with little conscious attention. However, conceptualisations of this vary in the literature (e.g. Moors & De Houwer, 2006) and it is often identified through its component parts and how it functions (Keatley et al., 2015). For the most part, functioning in this way is perfectly fine, and as we are doing so subconsciously it may be that we are not storing new memories as effectively as we would normally. This means that we feel we have no knowledge of what occurred on that particular journey.

So, whilst you never had an accident and are thus feeling proud of yourself, did it occur to you that you may have been lucky. What would have happened if that erratic driver would have jack-knifed his lorry across the carriageway and blocked your route? Do you think you would have been prepared? Perhaps averting this traffic incident would not be a sub-conscious response because it would require a variation from the norm. How aware, then, do you think your conscious brain is on a journey where you are functioning on autopilot? Perhaps our consciousness is aware of the journey but is not storing new memories. Could this mean that we could take decisive action if needed? It is generally agreed that we use both conscious and automated actions when we are driving (Charlton & Starkey, 2011), and studies on road traffic incidents have suggested that failures in automaticity may have contributed to the outcomes (Stanton & Salmon, 2009). This means that our concentration is diluted. In a similar manner, the concept of multi-tasking disrupts our thinking process because it is distracting. Would it make sense to attempt to do all your to-do list items in one hit, for instance? Working systematically through a to-do list helps us to focus and this can result in a much more robust approach to dealing with each item.

Many years ago, I devised a visualisation strategy for achieving short-term goals. It is not a ground-breaking strategy, and the evidence for its success is personal to my close colleagues and me and thus anecdotal; nevertheless, I would like to share it with you.

Headroom

Firstly, devise a to-do list all for all those tasks you have but let's focus on the short-term ones first. The list helps you to clear your mind of distractions. If necessary, you can prioritise this list once it is complete by placing a number against each item. This is the preparation done so now to the exercise.

In your head, imagine a series of rooms. Perhaps you will picture it like a hotel corridor or a large house. The inside of each room represents a thought, activity or task that you need to address (see examples below).

- Prepare lessons for next week
- Book onto that conference or CPD event you've put off recently
- Arrange tutorials for several students
- Sit down with your manager and discuss your Ofsted strategy
- Brush up on your subject knowledge (you can explore the specifications for other examining boards as a starting point)
- Devise several strategies for embedding English and maths within your subject (see Allan, 2017).

To undertake one of your tasks you must enter the appropriate room and be sure to close the door behind you. Once in the room, you are only to deal with that particular task and no other tasks are allowed in that room. If you recall something that is missing off your list it can be allocated to another room. Should this item prove more pressing, however, you will need to leave the room you are in and enter the room you allocated for the new item. One room one task ensures full concentration, and once you have addressed your task you can leave the room and close the door. It is important to shut the door because this represents closure (at least for now because you can return to a room). When you are ready, you can move into another room to tackle another item. If you are standing in the lobby and there are several doors open, you will see all those unfinished tasks calling for your attention. This is a huge distraction and will likely prevent you from fully engaging with the task you are working on. As such, there should only ever be one door open, that which you are about to enter.

The point of this exercise is that you deal with a task fully and only leave the room when you finish it. In this way, you deal with it robustly so that you can shut it out of your head and concentrate on the next item. If done correctly, it will stimulate concentration and enable you to be thorough. And because you have a system, your brain will be better equipped to tackle new challenges. For outstanding items, your brain will learn through experience that you will deal with them eventually, and thus can temporarily ignore them.

The strength of this exercise lies in its effectiveness and simplicity. It promotes intensity and concentration towards a particular task which means that the work involved is thorough. It also enables closure as a task can be completed with the metaphorical closing of the door. This activity works well for me and I hope it does for you too.

There are obviously variations on this – for example, you can merely work off your to-do list, focussing on each item separately and ticking them off as you go along. However, the room analogy creates a sense of psychological control. You are not only systematically working your way through the tasks and achieving, you are also generating the correct state of mind and encouraging yourself to think logically and productively. The visualisation involved in this exercise is powerful and is thus an effective way of telling yourself that you are in control. Through perseverance with each task, the exercise develops resilience. The achievement of each item, and the successful closing of that particular door, generates confidence in dealing with difficult tasks from beginning to end. As such, it demonstrates that you can resume normality when you are under pressure by taking control of the problems that you are confident you can deal with.

The traffic system of to-dos

Having your to-do list is essential because it is your metaphorical chipping away of the mountain ahead of you as you work hard to return to your regular lifestyle. This system involves colour-coding the items and then dealing with the most important or difficult ones first. Using the traffic system, you categorise each one hierarchically as red, amber or green. Red items may either be of high importance or the most difficult to overcome, whilst green may mean an easy win. You can build your confidence by dealing with the green ones first, providing they are ranked in difficulty rather than importance, otherwise it is red first for priority.

Continuing the traffic system analogy, you should treat the one you are working on only. Often in traffic we only see the car in front. This is certainly the most important one, anyway, as you need to act in response to the movement of that car first. Experienced drivers are aware of cars in front of that one, of course, but they bear in mind that the behaviour of the one directly ahead will dictate how they respond. If your situation changes and the task is downgraded in importance, you may need to overtake this car or turn to follow another one. This is the traffic system of prioritisation and can be useful to help you focus your energy on what is most appropriate. The cars are your stressors and need to be dealt with in turn.

Switching on, switching off

Whilst teaching is not exactly a 9–5 job, in the sense that you will plan, mark, and deal with queries beyond these hours, there does need to be a point at which you cease to think about your role and discharge the pressures of the day. If you leave a mechanical device on all day, every day – for example your TV – you will more than likely find that after running at this pace for a while it will come to the end of its current life. This is a mechanical device. It does not need to sleep and yet it still has a shelf life. It won't last forever and may overheat or develop a fault through overrunning. Now, consider a similar impact on yourself. You are not a machine and yet you might think that you can go on and on, regardless of the impact on your health. Teaching is a stress-related profession (Education Support, 2020), and thinking consistently about your job is not healthy for your brain or your body (see Chapters 3 and 4). This is counterproductive to your resilience and will likely result in burnout.

Switching off allows you to reclaim control, to reassess your problem, and to devise a plan of approach for the next day. A major problem with teaching today (and the world, to some extent) is the 'New York' lifestyle (the Big Apple never sleeps). Accessing services online may seem amazing when you can't get to the office, or you find yourself needing something in an emergency outside of office hours, but there needs to be a balance. And both your body and your mind like routine. Answering emails at 11pm may seem fairly innocuous but this means that you are still working and your brain is in work mode, thus failing to rest to make sense of the day's events. And if you are also up early this leaves very little time to reflect on work because you seem to be constantly immersed in it. Most students are understanding and will respect your private time but you may need to reinforce this message if you have previously been responding to emails at unsociable hours.

By failing to switch off you are potentially setting yourself up for failure in your role. Of course, during the pandemic this has been particularly difficult, and students have needs beyond the academic support of the institution. But a balance is essential if you are to function optimally. Arguably, part of your job is to help young people become independent, autonomous learners, and hopefully your students will continue learning for life, so being able to step away from them at key points is also crucial for their development.

If that does not convince you to slow down, consider the position from a mercantile perspective. You probably agree that you are underpaid due to the many cuts in the sector over the last few years. However, it is perhaps further disconcerting to view this in terms of your hourly pay if you are regularly working every evening and weekend.

Finding a quiet place

Sometimes, the pressure of a situation can be burdensome and rather than be cajoled into doing something you really don't want to do – particularly something that is merely adding to your workload and stress levels – removing yourself from the situation is a good idea. This allows you time to reflect on the impact of taking on that extra burden. It also enables you to reconsider your response and to plan your rationale for refusing to do something, as opposed to being caught unprepared and thus accepting something that might later prove to be too much. Consider your role in how stressed you are and whether you could have taken moments here and there to reflect and to readjust. Are you to blame in any of this? If so, you can change those particular aspects. An admission of fault should not be equated with failure, however. Rather, it is a positive move as it means that you are addressing the situation honestly and accurately.

Your quiet place is where you switch off in the day for a short period whilst you refocus. It is not a skive by any means, but a necessary space in which you can put things into perspective. This will also help with your bigger task of 'shutting down' in the evening to recharge your batteries because it will tune your body into switching from *work mode* to *rest mode* when necessary.

Setting targets

Resilient people are those individuals who cope well and in order to do so need to be seeing success in what they are trying to do. If you plan well, allowing yourself plenty of time, and only undertake tasks that are within your capability (stretching yourself where possible, of course), then you will not set yourself up to fail. You will also discourage others from misjudging you as they will get a more realistic picture of who you are. If you set yourself tasks that are unrealistic and, for the most part, unachievable, then you will be known for your failures and that can be unfair. There will be expectations on you that are unfeasible and those placing them on you (if not on yourself) may be unaware of this. Many of us set goals that are unachievable at times because we are aspirational, or are looking to challenge ourselves, and that is understandable. But we have to be reasonable about our progress. If a goal is to be deemed unachievable it should be revised as soon as possible.

Of course, failing to achieve unrealistic goals is by no means the same as failing to achieve those goals that are within your grasp. You will be aware of how much effort you have put in and how much return you are likely to yield, and the more you grow to understand yourself the more you will be able to recognise that some goals were never going to have been achieved because they were poorly planned. Setting achievable and appropriate goals, particularly when you have a realistic perception of your capabilities, helps you to develop your confidence. Whilst failure can occur when we least expect it, you are more likely to be prepared and resilient if prior to this point you had achieved your goals.

References

Allan, D. (2017). *Teaching English and maths in FE: What works for vocational learners?* London: Sage.

Andrews, B.R. (1903). Habit. *The American Journal of Psychology*, 14(2), 121–149. doi:10.2307/1412711

Brookfield, S. (1998). Critically reflective practice. *Journal of Continuing Education in the Health Professions*, 18(4), 197–205. https://doi.org/10.1002/chp.1340180402.4

Charlton, S.G. & Starkey, N.J. (2011). Driving without awareness: The effects of practice and automaticity on attention and driving. *Transportation Research Part F: Traffic Psychology and Behaviour*, 14(6), 456–471.

Davies, K.J.A. (2016). Adaptive homeostasis. *Molecular Aspects of Medicine*, 49, 1–7. https://doi.org/10.1016/j.mam.2016.04.007

Education Support (2020). *Teacher wellbeing index 2020*. Education Support. https://www.educationsupport.org.uk/sites/default/files/teacher_wellbeing_index_2020.pdf

Keatley, D.A., Chan, D.K.C., Caudwell, K., Chatzisarantis, N.L.D. & Hagger, M.S. (2015). A consideration of what is meant by automaticity and better ways to measure it. *Frontiers in Psychology*, 5, 1–3. https://doi.org/10.3389/fpsyg.2014.01537.

Moors, A. & De Houwer, J. (2006). Automaticity. *Psychological Bulletin*, 132(2), 297–326.

Peterson, J. (2019). *12 rules for life: An antidote to chaos*. Harmondsworth, UK: Penguin.

Stanton, N.A. & Salmon, P.M. (2009). Human error taxonomies applied to driving: A generic driver error taxonomy and its implications for intelligent transport systems. *Safety Science*, 47(2), 227–237.

Willingham, D.T. (2021). *Why don't students like school?* 2nd edn. London: Jossey-Bass.

7 Efficiency

Work smarter, not harder

If you find yourself in a position where you can no longer cope, you may need to look for the gaps in your timetable. This is not just your teaching timetable, it also relates to any time periods in your daily routine that you could utilise more effectively. A solid approach to any demanding situation is to map out exactly what you do against what you are expected to do to identify the areas of tension and your capacity for growth. Outlining your activities for each hour of the day will enable you to scope the potential for using your time wisely. Whilst this seems like a laborious audit of your time, it is not intended for draconian institutions to squeeze more out of you; rather, it is for you to reclaim some lost time and to become more efficient so that *you* can reap the benefits. If you feel that you are working to capacity, progress is perhaps about working smarter rather than harder.

In the example below, Rhonda, an English teacher in a college in the south of England recorded her activity over a typical week.

The darker shaded areas represent teaching or teaching-related activities whilst other times are for meetings, planning and marking, and student support. You will see that there are not many times where Rhonda can plan during her normal working hours and she has identified periods in her own time where she is working. Rhonda used this exercise to help her when she became overwhelmed and needed to find a way of returning to a more plausible and acceptable workload. Rhonda was surprised that she had some time in the morning that she could use more effectively. In her own words, she said …

> I wasn't sure what this was going to achieve. I know what I do each day, or at least I thought I did, and I didn't think there was any capacity to take on any more. I wasn't coping as it was, and I was really stressed with it all. I was on the verge of going off ill because it was all too much for me. But then I noticed gaps in my day where I could do things. I got in early because of the parking but I wasn't really using this time effectively before my day started. I would also take work home with me in the evening, so I was working very long days. Writing out what I do helped me to highlight all the times I was wasting. I have started planning when I get in and catching up on my

DOI: 10.4324/9780367824211-9

Table 7.1 Rhonda's timetable

Time and day	06:00–07:00	07:00–07:30	07:30–08:30	08:30–09:00	09:00–11:00	11:00–12:00	12:00–13:00	13:00–14:00	14:00–15:00	15:00–16:00	16:00–17:00	17:00–17:30	17:30–18:00	18:00–20:30
Mon	Breakfast and shower	Travel to work	Coffee and catch-up with colleagues	Set up teaching space	Teaching	Teaching	Teaching	Lunch	Teaching	Teaching	Teaching	Admin	Travel home	Dinner / Marking and/or lesson planning
Tues	Breakfast and shower	Travel to work	Coffee and catch-up with colleagues	Set up teaching space	Teaching	Teaching	Teaching	Lunch	Teaching	Teaching	Teaching	Admin	Marking and/or lesson planning	Travel home / Dinner / Leisure time
Wed	Breakfast and shower	Travel to work	Coffee and catch-up with colleagues	Set up teaching space	Teaching	Teaching	Teaching	Lunch	Marking and/or lesson planning	Marking and/or lesson planning	Marking and/or lesson planning		Travel home	Dinner / Leisure time
Thur	Breakfast and shower	Travel to work	Coffee and catch-up with colleagues	Admin	Student support	Team meeting	Marking and/or lesson planning	Lunch / Set up teaching space	Teaching	Teaching	Teaching	Admin	Travel home	Dinner / Marking and/or lesson planning
Fri	Breakfast and shower	Travel to work	Coffee and catch-up with colleagues	Set up teaching space	Teaching	Student support	Student support	Lunch	Student support	Admin		Travel home		Dinner. Leisure time
Sat						Marking and/or lesson planning								
Sun										Marking and/or lesson planning				

marking. I know it's not ideal starting work at 7:30 but, let's face it, if I'm in anyway I might as well be working. I grab myself a breakfast tea and take my time. I've also kept Friday mornings free for planning with colleagues. I think it's important to meet up, otherwise we all work in our silos. And it's good to talk when you're under a lot of pressure. The best part is that I get to go home and relax every night, so it's worked out well for me.

Rhonda is still working long hours but her newly revised timetable gives her something in return, and this has enabled her to reclaim some of her social life and leisure time in the evening. Rhonda also states that her sleeping pattern has improved and this has endowed her with greater quality of life. Rhonda takes the final word on this:

> I feel like I did when I first came into teaching. I mean, it was tough back then 'cos I was still learning. But I loved it. My situation's not perfect but doing this has certainly helped me to get through a very stressful period in my life. My next step now is to speak to the head of department about the number of hours I'm working. I'm not too hopeful with that one as I can't see her letting me go early just because I'm in at half seven. But it's made me feel like I'm back in the running again.

Vicarious development

Resilience will not take away your problems but it will help you to understand them better, to put them into context, and to devise a suitable strategy for dealing with them. Stressors are often difficult to measure objectively; rather, it is their impact on you and how you manage them that is more readily seen. Fortunately, however, much of this is within your control. Resilience helps us to keep an open mind and to adopt a perspective that categorises each stressor appropriately. The more resilient you are, the more you can handle change and can deal with complex situations. This is essential because life is complex and involves many, often uncomfortable, changes. We become more resilient when we have repeatedly encountered and survived difficult situations. Of course, this is not a recommendation to unnecessarily experience traumatic events in your life. But it is useful to learn from life experiences, of which there are usually many. You should also look for healthier ways of achieving a similar experience. One such way is through vicarious endeavours. Vicarious experiences will enable you to develop your empathy and can facilitate more objective thinking. Let's look at a scenario to see how this plays out.

Scenario

Your friend and colleague, Karen, is undergoing a divorce from her husband and is under extreme pressure from both her husband and his solicitors to sell the house they jointly own. As you do not personally have this pressure, you will probably be a little more clear-headed and hopefully on hand for good advice. However, Karen is a close friend that you have grown to love as a surrogate sister, and you are hurt by what she is going through. You may find it difficult to imagine how she is coping; even the fact that she seems able to smile when she comes to work can seem unusual. You talk to Karen and she appears to have a clear plan for moving her life forward. Notwithstanding the fact that she is the one undergoing the trauma, it is you who, when you put yourself in her situation, are unsure how you would ever move on from it. Karen is strong and resilient, and although she is suffering she will get through this so you can learn a lot from her (as well as simultaneously supporting her, of course).

Perhaps you never imagined Karen to be so strong and find her behaviour to be inspirational. You are now beginning to see the power of resilience in action. Karen refuses to let her problems prevent her from succeeding in life and despite all of this, and to your amazement, she has also applied for a promotion in your college. Your first impression is that this is a mistake for Karen. How could she take on a promotion with everything that is going on her life? However, Karen plans to use the promotion as an opportunity for a clean start and an apt distraction. She also utilises her divorce as a springboard for change, convincing herself that her husband was actually holding her career back.

Commentary

This approach works for Karen. She is drawing her energy from the situation and turning the negative experiences into opportunities. You may not want to replicate her attitude, of course, but you can take from it that there may be opportunities locked away in seemingly negative situations. Karen may be hiding, or even running away from, her emotions, and it is possible that the grieving process will set in at a later date, but this is her way of dealing with the situation. She also knows that by the time her delayed grieving sets in she will have already transformed the pattern of her life and convinced herself that a return to her old ways is both unproductive and of no use to her in her new life. Karen agreed to sell her house but only on her terms. She suggested that it is an opportunity to live somewhere else and to make a new start – new job, new home and, eventually, a new relationship. Karen's strength is admirable and there is much to extract from her situation. This is not about accepting a harsh situation, however; rather, it is about dealing with it in a much more efficient manner. Karen's response to the situation in no way demeans her experiences as she is in control throughout. Vicariously, then, you can develop your resilience through identifying some of the ingredients of Karen's approach that are successful and using these as a recipe for encountering future situations. You can learn to put your own position into context by learning about the situation of your friend, and this is something we do a lot of in life.

In the 1950s, Leon Festinger's social comparison model proposed that 'people evaluate their opinions and abilities by comparison respectively with the opinions and abilities of others' (Festinger, 1954, p. 118). In this way, an individual needs to situate herself within the structure of society and where she is placed will determine how she will behave. However, she will only compare herself to those she feels are of a similar ilk. In practice, this can be seen to play out with career comparisons. Teachers often compare themselves to other teachers, even if the subject they teach is radically different, because teaching itself provides a communal foundation. We can thus use Karen's experience to compare with how we would behave in that situation. Karen refuses to let the situation dictate an outcome for her and instead takes control of it. Her attitude is therefore facilitating her successful return to normality (or enabling her to outline a new normality). However, there may be aspects of Karen's ambition that some of us cannot relate to. Promotion, for instance, is not something that everyone aspires towards. As such, the successful reconstruction of a vicarious experience would depend on identifying only the relevant elements of it.

An alternative situation could be one in which you can demonstrate a resilient approach as you have an objective perspective on it. Let's suppose Karen is struggling to deal with her problem. Part of the strength for your resilience is generated through the gulf between Karen and you. That is, you do not become embroiled in her situation because of the distance you have between yourself and the problem. You may even propose a solution that you would never have been able to have thought of had it been you in that situation. Vicarious experiences in this way are not just helpful for your colleague, they also enable you to think about how you would respond, should you find yourself in a similar situation. In sum, you can learn from other people through supporting them and giving advice, or by eliciting a strategy from observing and talking to them about their experiences.

It is often difficult to find your inner strength when you are immersed in a situation and distance provides clarity and objectivity. If you have never come across a situation you can draw on, you might be able to find remnants of other situations that you can salvage and reuse. All experiences are potentially meaningful. Ask yourself, 'what is similar in this situation to events that have happened to me previously? What resources can I draw on to help with the current challenge?' In some situations, you may need to create your own resources. But if you are creative, there is usually something from some experience that you've had that you can relate it to. And even if this gives you confidence alone, it can be enough to prepare you for what lies ahead.

Don't be afraid to ask for help

This is a key feature of success as it means you can identify and acknowledge your constraints. Once you are aware of your limitations, you can become more resilient because you avoid setting yourself up to fail. Most people ask for help at some time in their life and many do so regularly. Not only is this acceptable behaviour, it is admirable and demonstrates more strength than weakness. It also displays confidence in your ability as it shows that you have a realistic perspective of what you are capable of. We all have weak areas but when we try to hide these – mostly for fear of exposure or through negative social comparisons – we become less resilient. We are also less able to survive an event if we feel ill-equipped. If we acknowledge this as an area for development, therefore, and focus only on the aspects of a situation that we can change, we are less likely to suffer the effects of not being prepared.

Sometimes we do not ask for help because we are surrounded by people who take more from us than give to us, and that is a typical situation for strong individuals. Asking for help can be daunting and you may feel it weakens you in some way. But the truth is that you will be much stronger in the long run. The thinking that there is strength in numbers (said to be attributed to Mark Shields (BrainyQuote, 2021)) is simple yet powerful in many circumstances. Great battles have been won purely on numbers, even where the odds are otherwise in favour of the opposing side.

Expanding your vicarious potential

Whilst we often think of resilience as an individual attribute, a feature within ourselves that sees us through difficult times, this can be limiting. Resilience requires a connection to the world through friends, family, and work colleagues, and the stronger those relationships are the more potential we have for demonstrating resilience. The old adage of 'a problem shared is a problem halved' has much to offer for resilience-building. According to the Phrase Finder (2020), it has been traced to an article in November 1931 in an English newspaper called the *Morecambe Guardian*. The article suggested that England in the 1930s was a period of gritty determinism and stiff upper lips, where people engaged in powerful, collaborative problem-solving. Indeed, between 1939 and 1945 there are many, many stories of heroism and stalwart individuals who have recomposed themselves against tremendous odds. These stories often involve ordinary people trapped in horrendous situations and exhibit the heroes and heroines who suffered greatly.

Of course, wars are horrific, destructive, and senseless, but from many traumatic events there have been survivors, and accompanying them, amazing tales of resilience and coping in the face of an apparently futile existence. In *Man's Search for Meaning*, Victor Frankl presents a difficult (yet impressive) narrative of one man's fight for survival against the odds. This is noted as a 'difficult' because of the nature of the suffering, but it is worth persevering through his account because, despite its ability to conjure up traumatic thoughts and unwanted human emotions, it is enlightening and inspirational. It is a story that needed to be told. Such trauma is a real part of life and should at the very least be acknowledged. Of course, the first message that we should take from any such text as this is that it must never happen again. But this perhaps goes without saying and Frankl's story is much more meaningful than that. For resilience-building, it is an amazing account of what can be achieved in some of the most extreme situations experienced by humans.

Dealing with trauma

Trauma is often associated with an injury or at least some form of shock to the body. But this does not always emanate from an accident. Sometimes it is the emotional aftereffects of a tragic event in our lives, such as losing a loved one, yet sometimes our working lives can also generate a traumatic experience. Trauma takes its toll on the body and when we are immersed in it we struggle to think clearly. It is often easier to advise others, or to support them in their hour of need, but doing this for ourselves can be extremely difficult. This is because of the judgement we place on ourselves. As mentioned above, if we treat our situation as though it was someone else's, we can begin to think objectively in order to devise a strategy for moving on. This can work well for situations we find ourselves in when we are alone.

For work-related situations, it is not advisable to spend too much time on thinking if there is no plan in place. That is, reflection is a necessary part of the recovery process, but it has to be balanced with the forming of your plans because resilience is about moving forwards. In situations such as facing redundancy, it is useful to take a little time out to gather your thoughts and to deal with the potential trauma of the experience. However, you should try to combine this reflection with positive thinking, and, if possible, the forming of a strategy for your next career step. For instance, perhaps the redundancy money will provide an income for a few months while you find another job, or it may kickstart you into

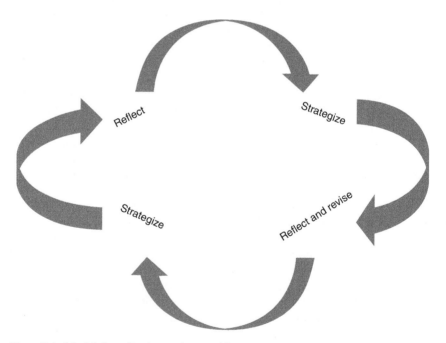

Figure 7.1. Model for reflecting and strategising

initiating that business venture you've long dreamed of. A good strategy is to reflect on your situation (take time out to compose yourself), form a plan (or identify a series of opportunities, if possible), and then reflect again on the suitability of the plan, revising it where necessary. The process is cyclical because you need to develop your plan as you go along yet continually consider the many factors involved. For instance, what will the plan lead to? Is it thorough? What are the pitfalls? What timeline should you align to implementing your plan? Who else is involved? A model for your reflecting and strategising can be seen in Figure 7.1.

Alcohol, the poor substitute

Without doubt, teaching is a stressful profession and there are many who leave within the first few years (Education Support, 2020; National Education Union, 2018). For others, perseverance is important as they want to make a success of what they have started. These people find their inner strength to continue because they love the profession and can clearly see the highly rewarding aspects, such as the many lives that have been transformed as students progress into successful careers and fulfil their aspirations (see UCU (2021) for various accounts of the wonderful impact FE can have on individual lives).

When under pressure, some teachers may feel that they need a 'crutch' – some manner of support to see them through – and there are obviously beneficial and destructive crutches you can draw on. Alcohol has received a mixed press coverage over recent decades as a result of varied (and conflicting) research findings (e.g. Brust, 2010; Goldberg et al., 2001; Holahan et al., 2010) but it is generally agreed that it is acceptable in moderation. However, it should never be used as a coping mechanism as it can be addictive and damaging to our health. Whilst a glass of wine each day may offer some benefits (depending on which study you choose to go with), it can become the norm to use this as your stress alleviator if unchecked. Moreover, as your stress grows, so too will the need to indulge. The phrase, 'not on a school night' is often used by teachers to resist this indulgence because they are aware of the potential slippery slope it offers. However, such good practice should be upheld beyond school nights as this attitude can lead to binge drinking at the weekend.

We all have our own perspective on everyday drugs such as alcohol and caffeine, and moderation is obviously the key. But the central message from this is that these should not become the regular release you draw on after a stressful day. Although they offer escapism, this is a temporal measure and you are merely masking your problems rather than facing them. Dealing with the small, day-to-day problems can equip us with the strength and resolve to tackle the wider, more important, issues. Small steps over time can result in much progress and can mitigate larger concerns. When you choose to ignore the smaller stressors, their significance can expand. Overall, alcohol is a poor resource for building resilience. It is a temporary distraction for your mental state but it has long-term effects that can grossly undo the effects of this distraction.

References

BrainyQuote (2021). Mark Shields' quotes. BrainyQuote. https://www.brainyquote. com/quotes/mark_shields_226003

Brust, J.C. (2010). Ethanol and cognition: Indirect effects, neurotoxicity and neuroprotection: A review. *International Journal of Environmental Research in Public Health*, 7(4), 1540–1557. doi:10.3390/ijerph7041540

Education Support (2020). *Teacher wellbeing index 2020*. London: Education Support. https://www.educationsupport.org.uk/sites/default/files/teacher_wellbeing_index_ 2020.pdf

Festinger, L.A. (1954). A theory of social comparison processes. *Human Relations*, 7(2), 117–140.

Goldberg, I.J., Mosca, L., Piano, M.R. & Fisher, E.A. (2001). Wine and your heart: A science advisory for healthcare professionals from the Nutrition Committee, Council on Epidemiology and Prevention, and Council on Cardiovascular Nursing of the American Heart Association. *Circulation*, 103(3), 472–475. https://doi.org/10.1161/ 01.CIR.103.3.472

Holahan, C.J., Schutte, K.K., Brennan, P.L., Holahan, C.K., Moos, B.S. & Moos, R.H. (2010). Late-life alcohol consumption and 20-year mortality. *Alcoholism: Clinical and Experimental Research*, 34(11), 1961–1971. https://doi.org/10.1111/j.1530-0277.2010. 01286.x

National Education Union (2018). *NEU survey shows workload causing 80% of teachers to consider leaving the profession.* https://neu.org.uk/press-releases/neu-survey-shows-workload-causing-80-teachers-consider-leaving-profession

Phrase Finder, The (2020). The meaning and origin of the expression: A problem shared is a problem halved. The Phrase Finder. https://www.phrases.org.uk/meanings/a-problem-shared-is-a-problem-halved.html

University and College Union [UCU] (2021). Transforming lives. London: University and College Union. https://transforminglives.web.ucu.org.uk/

8 Moving forward

This chapter in looks at the future of resilience building for individuals and identifies some of the areas you can utilise to transform your confidence, develop your self-esteem, and tackle your challenges head on.

Revel in your achievements and work at your goals

It is important to have goals, but you should not let them destroy your motivation if you don't achieve some of them. Goals are there to help you to develop, not to illustrate to everyone how incredibly poor you are at doing something. Goals are endpoints of achievement and are important development tools, but they should be realistic. You will know from your own role that much teaching is target-driven and this has both positive and negative aspects. Your goals are your ultimate target, of course, but you will need to establish small targets along the way – in the form of objectives – in order to reach your end goal (aim). Whilst this is something you do regularly with your students – advocating the usefulness of SMART (specific, measurable, achievable, realistic, timely) targets, for instance – you will need to channel your experience towards self-development. Your goals should not only be about achieving something arbitrary, they should be active contributors to your resilience. The realistic aspect of SMART is useful because resilience is not about merely feeling that nothing can take you down in life – that is delusional. It is about acknowledging your weaknesses and developing them; and this can be difficult if your self-esteem is low. As such, you should find a healthy balance where you revel in your achievements yet set further goals. Black and Wiliam (Teachers Toolbox, 2021) promote a similar concept for giving feedback, entitled 'medals and missions.' This is the approach that should work well for you, too. That is, recognise when you have done well so that you can build your confidence and self-esteem, then identify areas for your development where you can really challenge yourself.

Where identifying weaknesses can seem exposing and an acknowledgement of flaws, focusing on achievements can have the opposite effect, and this should help to create your balance. Your achievements represent the occasions when you have succeeded so you should reward yourself in some way. If your

DOI: 10.4324/9780367824211-10

students have scored well in a formative assessment that you devised, then that is attributable to you as well as to their hard work. After all, the hammer comes down on you when they don't achieve so why wouldn't you share in their success?

Challenging ourselves

As mentioned throughout this book, the concept of resilience is not about merely toughening up and persevering when unreasonable demands are being made, but it is crucial that we accept our own role in situations to acknowledge when we are at fault. We must recognise that we can be at fault too as this strengthens our situation, adds credibility for when we challenge the system (or those abusing it), and improves our outlook. We learn to recognise our limitations and the rationale behind these, so that we can challenge, with confidence, poor decision-making and abusive practices. This enables us to become stronger and thus more resilient.

Whilst achieving our goals is commendable, it is important to remember that making an effort and persevering is also a worthy pursuit. Failure can be difficult to accept but it has enormous benefits. It can help us to become successful by filling in the gaps in our knowledge and skills; that is, if we are aware of what makes us fail then we can plan to succeed. Failure gives us a realistic picture of the world and it develops resilience because we learn from our mistakes. We do this by understanding what failure is and then challenging ourselves to avoid it, or by embracing it as a trial run. Resilience is about having accurate knowledge of what we can and cannot do and this enables us to fight back.

College culture: Creating a culture for resilience

How teachers experience stress in their role is often dependent on how they perceive the environment, and it is not uncommon for one person to change the dynamics significantly, often to the detriment of those around him. Unfortunately, if that person is in a position of authority, it becomes difficult (although not impossible) to relieve the pressures emanating from his actions. As we have seen, stress is something that varies as it is dependent on how we perceive a situation. Stress is often the internalisation of our workload into an unreasonable and immediate to-do list. It is the pressure we put on ourselves as we try to live up to external standards. Of course, identifying the cause of a problem and implementing a solution is fine on an individual basis, but this can be impracticable if changes need to be operationalised institutionally. Your institution should provide support as you develop your resilience.

An unreasonable manager may be under significant pressure but merely passing the pressure down the line is poor management. If we are treated badly this generates a tense environment in which to work. Good managers will be aware of this and they will know that merely offloading stress is counterproductive as it can lead to illnesses; a factor that is destructive in two ways. First, it impacts on the individual's health and her family's wellbeing. Second, if meeting the demands is a way for the institution to save money then in the long run staff absences will negate this.

If you are working through a difficult situation, your college environment and the attitudes of your colleagues will impact on you enormously. Your resilience can drastically reduce when you attribute failure to yourself, and at this time you may need the support of your colleagues and the institution. If your working environment is destructive, however, and detrimental to your position, then you should acknowledge that the difficulties you face in returning to your usual teaching role are beyond your control. Resilient individuals can struggle in toxic situations yet continue to build their resilience, but they respond specifically to what is within their capacity to change, and they challenge unreasonable demands. Doing this alone, however, is tough, and without support you may need to ask yourself how healthy your working environment really is for you.

Alternative employment

One alternative to working in such a demanding and unproductive culture is to seek a job elsewhere. But this is easier said than done if you love teaching because notwithstanding the variance in the quality of the workplaces, the best places to work are likely to be those where the only lecturers who are leaving are those heading off to retirement. As such, many teachers leave the profession merely to take up a role that involves less remuneration because they regard their health as more important than money (Worth et al., 2015). In some ways, this is obviously a wise choice, but it is one that has been unfairly forced on you. It is perhaps worth considering, however, that if your environment is toxic then money can only help you to a certain extent. Quality of life and contentment in your profession is worth much more to you in the long run. This is not running away by any means, and you should always challenge inequities and unscrupulous practices, but you should ask yourself whether this is really the environment you can be happy in. If it is one person who is causing you distress, it may be worthwhile to challenge this person's behaviours in some way. However, if your distress is related to the institution as a whole, it might prove beneficial for both your physical and mental health if you seek a healthier and more productive environment. Not all colleges are the same and how they function can vary widely. Ask around, if possible, utilising connections from your social networks, to gauge whether your experiences are reflective of other people's.

Resilience and aspiration

In order to succeed, we usually have to fail many times. Resilience helps us fail gracefully but also effectively because failure is seen as a step closer to success. We know there are wrong routes to take, sometimes because we have previously taken them, but also that we can learn from these routes. To continue the metaphor,

Dreams ————————➤ **Aspirations**————————➤ **Goals** ————————➤**Success**

Figure 8.1. The dream-to-success trajectory

imagine you are driving to an unknown destination. If you take a wrong turning you know that you just need to go back and try again or perhaps find an alternative route. This is your driving resilience. Being lost is stressful but it is probably fair to say that most people believe that they will eventually arrive at their destination. For other areas in life, however, it is often difficult to feel confident enough to believe that things will turn out the way we expect, even when we have a lot of control. Understanding why we can be resilient with some aspects of our life and not in others draws on a number of factors, such as experience, attitude and aspirations. If we are confident and aspire to achieve, and our attitudes are focused on doing so, setbacks are easier to overcome. Having realistic aspirations builds a framework for understanding and helps us to plan the appropriate route. Like the car journey, when we make a mistake we learn to see this as a temporary measure and thus try an alternative route. In order to ensure our aspirations can be realised, we need to set aspirational targets. It may be helpful to conceptualise it as seen in Figure 8.1.

Dreams are often unrealistic, or at least contain many components that rely on fortuity, but they help us to form realistic aspirations. If your dream is to lead and inspire others, you can move towards making this happen by identifying your aspiration. For instance, perhaps you wish to become a college principal one day. This is a realistic aspiration that fulfils your leadership dream, and it could translate well into a series of goals.

In the education world, we are used to setting targets and this can sometimes feel mechanistic. But achieving targets helps to build confidence and self-esteem as it illustrates to us that progress can and does occur. It is important when setting targets to stretch ourselves as learning can be more effective when we are challenged (Coe et al., 2014). This will develop resilience as it demonstrates to us that with commitment and perseverance we can overcome great hurdles. Aspirations, then, can sustain our momentum through difficult times by guiding us to where we want to be.

Box 8.1 Tips for becoming resilient

1   Get some perspective. What does this problem mean in real terms? What's the worst that can happen?

2   Compare the undeserved bad things that happen to you with those unearned good things that have happened? Life is about ups and downs.

3   Identify occasions of resilience. Think about the times when you have been strong and what it was that made you excel in that situation. Use the driving resilience analogy as a springboard for your thinking.

4　Identify your role and your capacity to act. You can't control every situation, but you can control how you react to them.

5　Focus on your power and not your helplessness. Work at the things you can change and accept the things you cannot, perhaps asking for help.

6　Accept that some suffering is part of human existence but seek ways to reduce this suffering where possible.

7　Ask yourself what contribution you have made to the situation (without arbitrarily assigning blame to yourself) so that you can address that particular aspect.

8　Decide whether what you are doing is helping the situation or harming you in any way?

9　Exercise and stay healthy. A healthy body is a healthy mind. Resilient individuals are made and not born. (Yes, genetics play a role, but these can also be developed through experience.)

10　Rest and recuperate. Form positive sleep patterns and have downtime and moments of self-indulgence.

11　Take regular breaks from the desk when not teaching.

12　Develop meaningful relationships. Loneliness can be harmful to both your physical and mental health. Studies show that those who live longer are usually in some form of happy relationship (Malone et al., 2013). Social connections are essential because we are social animals and 'human resilience depends on the richness and strength of social connections, as well as on active engagement in groups and communities' (Bzdok & Dunbar, 2020). Working collaboratively has helped us to survive and throughout history a pack mentality and tribalism have been key features for hunting and protection. *Together we are strong*, as the saying goes.

13　Exercise more. Surprisingly, doing more will actually give you more energy (see Chapter 4).

14　Engage in your hobbies (or non-work activities) to switch off from your role.

15　Distance yourself from a problem to approach it objectively. If possible, imagine that the problem is that of a friend's and you are merely providing advice.

16　Identify and track your stressors. Keep a stress journal for one month and this will help you to identify instances of stress and how you dealt with them.

17　Listen to your body. Don't ignore tiredness, for instance. This is a message to say that something is wrong and is a signal for forthcoming stress. You may be getting the right amount of sleep but what is the quality of this like? If you are lethargic, monitor your physicality as well as your sleep pattern.

18　Accept that change is a normal feature of life. For example, you have previously been a baby, a child, a teenager and so on.

19　If change is permanent, ask yourself what the new norm will look like and how long it will take you to adjust to it.

References

Bzdok, D. & Dunbar, R.I.M. (2020). The neurobiology of social distance. *Trends in Cognitive Sciences*, 24(9), 717–733.

Coe, R., Aloisi, C., Higgins, S. & Major, L.E. (2014). *What makes great teaching? Review of the underpinning research*. London: Sutton Trust. https://www.suttontrust.com/wp-content/uploads/2014/10/What-Makes-Great-Teaching-REPORT.pdf

Malone, J.C., Cohen, S., Liu, S.R., Vaillant, G.E. & Waldinger, R.J. (2013). Adaptive midlife defense mechanisms and late-life health. *Personality and Individual Differences*, 55(2), 85–89. https://doi.org/10.1016/j.paid.2013.01.025

Teachers Toolbox (2021). *Black and Wiliam 1998*. Teachers Toolbox. https://www.teacherstoolbox.co.uk/black-and-wiliam-1998/

Worth, J., Bamford, S. & Durbin, B. (2015). Should I stay or should I go? NFER analysis of teachers joining and leaving the profession. Slough, UK: National Foundation for Educational Research. https://www.nfer.ac.uk/publications/lfsa01/lfsa01.pdf

9   The importance of reflection

Introduction

This chapter emphasises the need for teachers to engage in deep and productive thinking in order to explore the complexity of a problematic situation, and to propose a constructive response. It demonstrates the power of greater self-awareness that can be gleaned from reflection and identifies effective use of it as a key component of resilience-building.

What is reflection?

It is important to begin this chapter by defining reflection, particularly in relation to resilience. Reflection is important and we learn a great deal when we reflect because things begin to make sense to us. Indeed, you may ask yourself, can we really learn anything without reflecting? Of course, this depends on how you conceptualise reflection. Thinking about something is necessary but reflection usually requires a little depth to our thinking. Reflection should also be meaningful; that is, it should move us towards a conclusion. It should be challenging and even encourage us to rethink our philosophy if necessary. As Finley (2018, p. 1185) suggests, reflection 'must be deliberate, sincere, and honest. It should force us to confront our egos and self-interests.' Reflection, then, is the process of cognitively grappling with problems, ideas and challenges in order to seek a resolution, and the better we are able to do this the more likely we are to develop resilience.

Reflection can develop resilience because it involves the deep thought processes that produce results, and this can help us to challenge our own outlook. Reflection is more than mere navel gazing, however. It is about exploring our inner thoughts to understand how we make sense of the world; it is about knowing where and how we are placed within a situation; it is about ensuring that our understanding is as comprehensive and as accurate as possible; it is about making connections between ideas and perspectives; and it is about finding ways forward once we fully understand a situation. Thus, reflection is often problem solving in the mind, and Lucas (1991, p. 84) interprets it as 'the systematic enquiry into one's own practice to improve that practice and to

DOI: 10.4324/9780367824211-11

deepen one's understanding of it.' In this way, reflection is an analytical and self-exploratory practice that is used to promote intellectual growth and professional development. Reflection thus utilises our experiences to influence our outlook and challenge our understanding and assumptions (Brookfield, 1998), and it is this flexible, yet bespoke, process that enables us to build resilience. That is, resilience helps us to cope with change and reflective practice encourages us to utilise it in order to progress.

Why reflect?

According to Wald (2015, p. 704), when forming a professional identity, 'Reflective skills enhance … resilience.' This is because reflection stimulates the analysis of a situation and the individual's role within it. As professionals, we become more self-aware through reflection and grow to understand how we function during stressful periods. This self-knowledge is important because it is often difficult to devise generic strategies for human development that involve in-depth understanding. You are the expert of You. You can hinder Your progress and achievement, but You can also facilitate opportunities for You to become successful. With this in mind, the more you know about yourself, the more effectively you can equip yourself to cope with change and thus deal with stressful situations.

We reflect so that we have a deeper understanding of our situation and this enables us to devise a strategy for how we will approach it. As Larrivee (2000, p. 294) points out:

> When teachers become reflective practitioners, they move beyond a knowledge base of discrete skills to a stage where they integrate and modify skills to fit specific contexts, and eventually, to a point where the skills are internalized enabling them to invent new strategies.

This is essential for resilience-building because we can stay in control. The more we know of a situation, and the more we have ownership of it, the better armed we can be to tackle it. Through reflection, we often discover answers to what we might initially deem irresolvable difficulties. Often, these problems need to be deliberated for some time, and one of the strengths of reflection is that it builds on previous thinking and forms new connections between old ideas and new ones. As we continue to reflect, we draw on new experiences and this can provide vital stimuli for revising our thought processes. Those eureka moments do not happen often, but they can and do happen as our thoughts reach a pinnacle. This is the power of reflection and it has been used by humans in various ways for thousands of years.

Sometimes, those who regularly think self-reflectively are referred to as narcissistic. This is perhaps due to the deep interest in themselves, and it emphasises the introverted and inward-looking approach that deep reflection requires. In Greek mythology, Narcissus is said to have fallen in love with his own reflection in a pool of water, although other sources suggest that 'to console himself for the death of his beloved twin sister, [he] sat gazing into the spring to recall her features' (Encyclopaedia Britannica, 2021, np). For reflection to be effective, however, it should involve criticality and the challenging of the self that goes beyond mere admiration. Reflection is arguably part of learning for life and it can be used to help us continue to develop throughout our careers.

Reflective models

Reflection has been a focus for education for many years and across many countries (Poom-Valickis & Mathews, 2013), and it is regarded as a productive strategy for professionals to engage in both self-analysis and self-evaluation. Reflection strengthens your ability to critique your performance and to identify areas for improvement, and there are many reflective models that you can explore to achieve effective reflective practice. You may have already encountered some of these if you have undertaken teacher training, but they are certainly worth revisiting, particularly with your newfound resilient outlook. Each model has its strength but also its limitations, and you will need to find which one resonates with you and your practice. It is thus worth exploring briefly some potentially useful models here. As this is a major field in its own right, however, the following is merely a potted account of selected theorists and their models.

Graham Gibbs

Gibbs' (1988) model of reflection comprises the following six stages of development:

1 Description
2 Feelings
3 Evaluation
4 Analysis
5 Conclusion
6 Action Plan

In *Description*, the details of the situation are outlined in a factual manner. No emotional connection is needed here as that takes us into the second stage, *Feelings. Evaluation* enables the individual to explore the strengths and weaknesses of the situation, whilst *Analysis* looks for the rationale behind these. During these stages it is also useful to bring in any relevant literature as *Analysis* is the stage in which understanding begins. In *Conclusion*, we make sense of the situation as a whole and any variances in understanding can be synthesised in this stage. Finally, the process requires applicability so an *Action Plan* is devised to identify its practical usage. Overall, this model is useful in that it guides the individual through a process and pinpoints what is needed in each stage.

Donald Schön

Schön's *reflection-in-action* and *reflection-on-action* is also a popular way to conceptualise our reflective processes in teaching because it is seemingly straightforward and thus appeals to busy teachers. However, we should not underestimate the potential for the complex thinking that these terms can stimulate as the complexity lies with the depth in which the individual engages with them. A simplistic understanding of these terms is the difference between reflecting in the moment – or, as Schön (1991, p. 54) describes this, 'thinking on your feet' – and reflecting after the moment has passed, such as after a teaching session has finished. However, Schön fails to acknowledge the concept of 'reflection-before-action' (Greenwood, 1993).

There are pros and cons for each approach. Reflection-in-action enables the teacher to immediately revise something that is not working, but a misjudgement on behalf of the teacher can result in unnecessary change to a lesson. Reflection-on-action allows for more objectivity as the teacher is no longer immersed in the class and may be able to form a more accurate understanding of what occurred. However, waiting until the lesson has finished may have resulted in lost opportunities for sustaining the students' interests. Clearly, a combination of approaches is needed and teachers are encouraged to reflect regularly. With experience, a teacher will be able to make some relevant decisions in class, responding to the needs of the students and the dynamics of the lesson, and thus either make changes or allow the lesson to continue as planned. As the teacher develops her relationship with the students, she will eventually be able to assess the situation more accurately. This will coincide with the development of her 'tacit knowing-in-action,' a skill whereby she can make judgements based on knowledge she has but may not be consciously aware of. Schön draws influence from Polanyi's (1958) 'tacit knowing' for this concept.

Stephen Brookfield

Brookfield's seminal paper in 1998, entitled "Critically Reflective Practice" advocates using a variety of perspectives to inform reflection. In it, he identifies the following lenses:

1   Our autobiography as a learner of practice
2   Our learners' eyes
3   Our colleagues' experiences
4   Theoretical literature.

This is a useful approach to reflection for teachers because it encourages them think about how a situation is perceived by others. It challenges the teacher to question his own assumptions and to consider how the multiple perspectives interrelate. The first category is based on the professional development of the teacher, utilising reflection to evaluate progress. The second category encourages the teacher to consider the perspective of the students. For example, the teacher may want to ask, 'Was that a motivating lesson? If I were a student in this class, what impression would I have of it?' We then move to the perspective of colleagues. If someone should walk in the classroom during the lesson, would they find it stimulating? Would they see the learners engaged? This is a little bit like the Hawthorne effect (French, 1953) in that people act differently when they know they are being observed and is perhaps a good strategy to take. After all, if you would not want your colleagues to see your lesson then you probably should be unhappy with it as well.

The final category looks at the literature and this is often underutilised in teaching. Research findings make their way to teachers through a wide variety of sources, and often it is invisible to them (Cain & Allan, 2017). It is necessary, then, to check out the origin of what we do at times to validate practices. Many myths have perpetuated education (e.g. Kirschner, 2017; Letrud & Hernes, 2016), sometimes through poor research or research findings that need much more exploration, but other times because the strategy in question evolves as it migrates and remains unchallenged.

The power of co-reflection

In building resilience, interactions with colleagues provide crucial platforms for contextualising difficulties and for sharing ideas. We can learn from our resourceful colleagues, and this puts our own thoughts into perspective. But we can also share our own ideas for reaffirmation, and our ideas can be challenged when we need to refocus. But more than this is the power of collaboration to generate new understandings. Sharing and discussing ideas, collaboratively planning, and challenging strategies is not merely about learning *from* your colleagues, it can facilitate a space to learn *with* them. The synthesis of your experiences, then, can lead to the co-construction of pedagogical knowledge (Allan, 2022).

A prominent coping mechanism within highly resilient individuals is the capacity for dealing with change. When we share problems, we seek reinforcement from others in that we gauge whether the problem is as difficult, and seemingly insurmountable, as we feel it is; as such, we embrace alternative perspectives. Moreover, it is sometimes easier for someone else to resolve a concern as there is an element of distance between them and the problem. Thus, you have a mixture of objectivity (reduced emotional involvement) and subjectivity. Providing the inputs are valid, this combination is a great recipe for synthesis. Through co-reflection, we open ourselves up to be challenged, and this can be daunting; however, it is arguably essential if we are looking to develop. Being challenged is difficult, but where it is constructive it is usually a worthwhile venture.

Collaborating in this manner engenders a culture of co-reflection, wherein colleagues' thought processes are shared before they are finalised. According to Yukawa (2006, p. 203), co-reflection is 'a collaborative critical thinking process mediated by language, broadly construed to include all meaningful signs.' Thus, knowledge is the resultant factor of an active process of dialogic engagement. This differs from the introspection of solitary reflection, and some who have engaged in co-reflection suggest it promotes greater criticality (Allan et al., 2020).

Reflection for change

As a tool for professional progress, reflection is flawed in that it is dependent on our perceptions and experiences. However, it can help us to engage with our performance as we gauge our abilities. As resilient individuals, we reflect on, and learn from, previous experiences. A stressful situation in teaching that might otherwise push us out of our comfort zone can make a positive contribution to our progress if we engage with reflection. If the situation is one we have encountered before, the level of familiarity should equip us to deal with it. If it is new to us, however, it may require a more innovative approach. In this instance, we look for recognisable aspects, or familiar patterns, that we can relate to because these are likely to be the parts of the problem that we are confident in dealing with.

To exemplify this, let us suppose you have been told about a restructure within the college, wherein many roles and workloads will likely change. However way you look at this it will have a negative impact somewhere down the line on someone, and you probably cannot change that. With your resilient head on, however, you will draw from your prior experiences of dealing with change and begin to ready yourself for the new world. This is not to suggest for one minute that you should offer no resistance, of course. And as stressed throughout this book, fighting unnecessary changes is essential in most situations. But if the fight is futile, and you know that you are constrained in what you can have an impact on, you may be left with the decision to either adapt or leave the college altogether.

Whatever you choose to do it is likely to require resilience due to the impact the change will have on you. You need strength to fight, adversity to adapt, and courage to leave. This is a difficult time that has been imposed upon you and it would be naïve to suggest that you can just challenge these changes should they arise. However, you should explore your options to see what you can challenge. Restructuring is a legitimate strategy that many organisations use and it is thus unusual for most employees to be in a position to stop it from occurring. It is not within the remit of this book to discuss the legality of such a situation, of course; suffice to say, it is always worth seeking advice from your union. But once your challenging capacity is exhausted (if it unfortunately gets to that stage), you may need to save your resilience for your new role.

Having taught across other programmes and other courses, you may have resilience to draw on to adapt to your change of job as you attempt to bring normality back to your life. For instance, you know from experience that whilst teaching a new subject requires many hours of groundwork in establishing and strengthening your core knowledge, it is not as daunting as it appears. If you have to apply for a new job, then, this change in your life may be stressful but it may also be a strategic career move. This is not giving up; it is about making the most appropriate decision for you. It is often difficult adapting to change, particularly if it seems to negate all your previous hard work, but it can sometimes prove necessary.

The sunk cost effect

The sunk cost effect is a commitment we make to seeing something through, regardless of how unlikely it is to succeed. It could be summed up in the famous words of Magnus Magnusson, a former presenter on the British television show, Mastermind (BBC, 2021) – 'I've started so I'll finish.' The term was proposed in 1985 by Hal Arkes and Catherine Blumer and was defined as 'a greater tendency to continue an endeavor once an investment in money, effort, or time has been made' (Arkes & Blumer, 1985, p. 124). However, there can be many negative consequences to such commitment. Continuing with a destructive path may be far more detrimental than cutting your losses and moving on; when we invest in something we usually expect a return. If not, this can be a bitter pill to swallow and we may feel compelled to continue until the investment pays off.

The sunk-cost effect represents a 'cognitive bias' and it is 'supported by evidence from laboratory-based, archival and field-based research in numerous fields' (Sirois, 2019, p. 398). It is a simplistic concept yet interestingly it appears to be an accurate depiction of how many humans succumb to the lure of investment. The term represents a metaphorical slippery slope that can destroy our confidence and cause us to resist deep reflective practice, particularly if it means denial of reality. Resilient individuals have perseverance yet adopt a realistic perspective, knowing when they can change a situation and accepting when they cannot. If we blame ourselves for failure, and we persist with a lost cause, this failure will magnify and our problems will be perpetuated, thus resulting in further feelings of incompetence. Confidence in our ability is essential for building resilience because we often face the unknown and thus need to trust in ourselves rather than in the situation.

Many people have found themselves prey to the sunk cost effect – perhaps they have invested a lot of time and effort in a particular career that is not progressing in the way they hoped. This can be extremely difficult, particularly if the investment represents a significant proportion of their life. For instance, if someone had completed a university degree, secured a job in their chosen career, undertaken many hours of training and other forms of professional development and so on, only to arrive at the decision that this career was not for them (see example), they would be understandably frustrated. Such a situation can impact hugely on self-esteem and confidence, even if it is the right action to take. It is difficult not to feel like a failure when plans go awry but fixating on negativity will not change the situation. However, if change is possible, reflection can equip us to identify how this might be achieved and thus arm us with resilience. If we lack resilience, moving on from a situation is difficult. Not only is there the investment that must now be discarded, there is also the angst that significant change and a fear of the unknown can instil.

Box 9.1 Case study

John left university with a degree in archaeology, and an avid interest in history, and volunteered to work on a number of excavations in order to build up his practical experience. Whilst doing this, he applied for a variety of archaeological-related positions in order to pursue his dream career. However, the jobs were few and far between and after moving around the country for several years he decided on a career change. This was an incredibly difficult decision for John because he had invested many years in his training, both at university and beyond, and now had to tell himself that it was time for a career change. John struggled to adapt because he felt that the decision had been taken out of his hands. He grappled with his thoughts for a number of months as he took on low-paid work to sustain him.

At this stage, John had convinced himself that he was a failure, and that the reason his career path had not been laid out in the manner in which he expected was because of his incompetence. In many ways, he fell into a fixed mindset at this stage (see Chapter 2) and came to the conclusion that archaeology was not for him because he was 'not cut out for it.' From hereon, John became depressed. He struggled with the conflict that arose from his belief that he had failed in his career but that it was also too late to move to another one. He returned to archaeology again and again over the next five years but could only source unpaid work, probably due to a lack in confidence and motivation. John was frustrated as he believed he was not good enough to become an archaeologist but felt that having invested so much of his life working towards this goal, he could not do anything else.

In some ways, his commitment seems honourable as he is persevering in the face of adversity and thus might initially be perceived as resilient. However, his lack of belief in himself was destroying his resilience and he was persevering solely to avoid change, rather than embrace it. As such, John became trapped in a self-made rut. As his confidence dropped, so too did the number of voluntary hours he undertook on various sites. John enrolled on a training course to secure a licence with the Security Industry Authority (SIA), then sought a role in a museum. He was not interested in the role itself, however, merely the fact that it was in a museum and that he could tell himself he was not a failure in archaeology as he retained a connection to it, albeit tenuous. Unfortunately, at this stage, John's original passion for archaeology was long gone, yet he felt he needed to continue linking to the industry in some way. He describes how he began to hate archaeology but could not bring himself to do anything else.

Commentary

John was a victim of many things – cognitive dissonance, self-fulfilling prophecy, for instance – and now the sunk cost effect as he could not progress beyond his initial investment. 'I don't want to waste my degree,' he stated.

We could analyse this situation in many ways – e.g. perceiving John's pursuit for success as an archaeologist as admirable or identifying the problem as his lack of faith in himself – but the sunk cost effect is arguably strong. Whether John should have chosen another career or persisted in a more determined and positive manner is perhaps personal choice, but the added factor of being miserable from his efforts suggests that his investment was misguided, and that he missed an opportunity to excel in a second career. Deep down, however, John merely wanted a career. And whilst this was not specific to archaeology, he felt that he was trapped and had already made his career choice. However, many people in today's society have two, three, and sometimes more careers over their working life. How this is conceptualised, then, can be important for building resilience. Making informed choices as an individual can be empowering, and with greater resilience John may have been in a stronger position to shut out the past and pursue another career.

Reflection helps us to be critical of ourselves but we have to be ready to admit when change is needed. In the sunk cost effect, we often persevere with a concept/strategy etc. because we feel that it's too difficult to turn back. Through reflection – particularly using a reflective model as this encourages objectivity – we learn to get to know ourselves better and to take a stronger, more critical, stance on our situation. We can draw from our experiences, then, as these often shape how we think; but it would be unproductive to allow these experiences to limit our progression and, as seen with John, to make us unhappy. Fortunately, this example has a happy ending as John is now working in a secondary school teaching history, but it may well have ended worse had he not have been able to eventually move on from his fixation to 'finish what he had started.'

The problem of poor reflection

It is often difficult to reflect deeply when you need to challenge yourself. As Larrivee (2000, p. 295) suggests, 'shedding a dearly-held belief shakes our very existence.' However, it is important to be self-critical if we are to develop to the best of our ability. Reflection is a powerful tool but when used superficially it can be useless and even damaging. Busy professionals often struggle to reflect effectively, particularly in the moment, and thus fail to take time to fully appreciate its effectiveness. For instance, how often do great ideas jump into our heads? Even when these ideas seemingly do so they are usually built on the back of hours or days (even months and years) of subconscious thinking about our situation. When we feel that time is against us, reflective practice is all too easily applied in bland, mechanical, and unthinking ways (Boud & Walker, 1998).

If we deny the complexity of our roles as teachers, and fail to engage in reflective thinking that is transformational, we commit a huge disservice to our professional practice. It is not enough to merely think, 'that was a tricky situation, I'm glad it's over.' We must go beyond this superficiality to deconstruct the event and thus identify the key components that ensure success (often by identifying the elements that bring failure). This can be done using a reflective model and doing so this builds character and develops meaningful experiences that we can utilise as we develop resilience for our next problematic encounter. This aspect of resilience, then, is based on preparedness so that we may 'spring back' to normality more effectively.

References

Allan, D. (2022). Lesson Study and teacher training: Engaging in the co-construction of pedagogical knowledge. In E. Sengupta & P. Blessinger (Eds.), *Innovative approaches in pedagogy for higher education classrooms*. Bingley, UK: Emerald.

Allan, D., Pham Hoai, A. & Le Nu Cam, L. (2020). East meets West: Exploring the challenges of cross-cultural collaboration in pedagogical development. In C. Woolhouse & L. Nicholson (Eds.), *Mentoring in higher education: Case studies of peer learning and pedagogical development* (pp. 215–234). Cham: Palgrave Macmillan.

Arkes, H.R. & Blumer, C. (1985). The psychology of sunk cost. *Organizational Behavior and Human Decision Processes*, 35(1), 124–140. doi:10.1016/0749-5978(85)90049-90044

BBC (2021). *Mastermind*. https://www.bbc.co.uk/programmes/b006mk1s

Boud, D. & Walker, D. (1998). Promoting reflection in professional courses: The challenge of context. *Studies in Higher Education*, 23(2), 191–206. doi:10.1080/03075079812331380384

Brookfield, S. (1998). Critically reflective practice. *Journal of Continuing Education in the Health Professions*, 18(4), 197–205. https://doi.org/10.1002/chp.1340180402.4

Cain, T. & Allan, D. (2017). The invisible impact of educational research. *Oxford Review of Education*, 43(6), 718–732. doi:10.1080/03054985.2017.1316252

Encyclopaedia Britannica (2021). Narcissus. https://www.britannica.com/topic/Narcissus-Greek-mythology

Finley, R.S. (2018). Reflection, resilience, relationships, and gratitude. *American Journal of Health-Systems Pharmacy*, 75(16), 1185–1190. doi:10.2146/ajhp180249

French, J.R. (1953). Experiments in field settings. In L. Festinger & D. Katz (Eds.), *Research Methods in the Behavioral Sciences* (pp. 98–135). New York: Dryden Press.

Gibbs, G. (1988). *Learning by doing: A guide to teaching and learning methods*. Oxford: Oxford Further Education Unit.

Greenwood, J. (1993). Reflective practice: A critique of the work of Argyris and Sch6n. *Journal of Advanced Nursing*, 18, 1183–1187.

Kirschner, P.A. (2017). Stop propagating the learning styles myth. *Computers & Education*, 106, 166–171. doi:10.1016/j.compedu.2016.12.006

Letrud, K. & Hernes, S. (2016). The diffusion of the learning pyramid myths in academia: An exploratory study. *Journal of Curriculum Studies*, 48(3), 291–302. doi:10.1080/00220272.2015.1088063

Larrivee, B. (2000). Transforming teaching practice: Becoming the critically reflective teacher. *Reflective Practice*, 1(3), 293–307. doi:10.1080/713693162

Lucas, P. (1991). Reflection, new practices and the need for flexibility in supervising student teachers. *Journal of Further and Higher Education*, 15(2), 84–93.

Polanyi, M. (1958). *Personal knowledge: Towards a post-critical philosophy.* Chicago, IL: University of Chicago Press.

Poom-Valickis, K. & Mathews, S. (2013). Reflecting others and own practice: An analysis of novice teachers' reflection skills. *Reflective Practice*, 14(3), 420–434.

Schön, D.A. (1991). *The reflective practitioner.* Aldershot, UK: Ashgate.

Sirois, L.P. (2019). The psychology of sunk cost: A classroom experiment. *The Journal of Economic Education*, 50(4), 398–409. doi:10.1080/00220485.2019.1654954

Wald, H.S. (2015). Professional identity (trans)formation in medical education. *Academic Medicine*, 90(6), 701–706. doi:10.1097/ACM.0000000000000731

Yukawa, J. (2006). Co-reflection in online learning: Collaborative critical thinking as narrative. *International Journal of Computer-Supported Collaborative Learning*, 1, 203–228.

Part 3

Stories of resilience

10 Case study

Paul's story

I was made redundant due to a college merger back in 2015. I was in the smaller institution so we were seen as the underdog. The powers that be told us we would all keep our jobs, so we believed them. I'm not naïve, but you put your trust in people, don't you? Especially when they make out that you're valuable and the college couldn't operate without you. I was involved in all the excursions – I used to take students out to the cinema or to film locations. It was a great experience and it helped us all to bond. I got on well with the head of department and I was respected throughout the college. The people I worked with joked that the college had been built around me because I'd been there so long. One colleague even said that they should have a care home built in so that I could retire and stay on site. A bit silly, but it showed that they cared. Anyway, I was firmly entrenched in the college so when it came it knocked me for six. 'There's going to be a restructure,' they said. 'Some of your roles will have to change, slightly, and once we're properly merged there'll be a job of assimilation to do.'

I wondered what that meant at first and then the penny dropped: either you're in or you're out. So, it became clear that some of us were going to lose our jobs – jobs that we'd worked really hard in for years, with many long days and unpaid hours that had excessively driven us into the ground. But I didn't mind because teaching was my life. It didn't matter that I often worked in the evenings or came into college in the summer holidays. I'd even spend my weekend at a conference or CPD event, sometimes, because this was about me and my career. I was proud to say that I was an educator and a film studies scholar.

The first 'call' was for voluntary redundancies, but nobody was interested in leaving or was even close enough to retirement to consider it. Stalemate? Not quite. The game was not yet over. 'Last one standing' was more like it. I guess I was a big fish in a little pond because during the merger I suddenly found my identity challenged. It was one of the most stressful experiences I've had. I put my life into this career and all of a sudden it was slipping away from me. I didn't know what to do because I didn't have a back-up. I also didn't have much else in my life because I was fixated on the world of film studies. I'm passionate about it, I'm a member of several film networks. I also subscribe to an online film magazine and have written a couple of articles for it. When the news came that there were to be redundancies, I don't think I realised that

DOI: 10.4324/9780367824211-13

everything I stood for, that I'd worked hard for, could come crashing down. Part of me was arrogant and refused to believe it, perhaps I didn't want to. I ignored it, thinking it would go away, but was wrong to do so. This meant that I was in no position to deal with what was to come and it hit me hard.

After I left the college, my attitude deteriorated, and I became overly focused on trying to resume my former lifestyle. I fought to get my job back but that was futile so I scoured the job market to see what could replace this huge gap in my life. I was interviewed for a couple of colleges but in retrospect I could see that my attitude was now so awful they were probably shocked to see the dissonance between my CV, with all its richness in qualifications and exuding passion and experience, and the me that turned up in person. My enthusiasm had gone and I didn't believe this job could replace my old one, so I flunked it. I took to drinking to ease the pain and my problems were 'put on hold' from around noon each day. Deep down, I knew this was not the answer. But I was in a rut and, ironically, not getting another job made me feel even more insecure.

The stark reality resurfaced every morning, compelling me to recommence the destructive cycle of my alcoholic venture. I think I was a functioning alcoholic, and at one stage the only end in sight was one I refused to contemplate at such a young age (I was barely into my forties). I was depressed and suffered with severe anxiety. My relationship broke up and my wife left me. I was at rock bottom and a visit to the doctor resulted in anti-depressants, which I started taking immediately. I'm not sure what impact these had on me, though. I felt better at first but then a lot worse when they kicked in, so I stopped taking them. I think they were masking my problem rather than encouraging me to take stock of my life.

The months rolled by and I found myself becoming more of a victim, believing I would never get back on my feet. I needed professional help. I tried to understand my situation and what had led up to it. Why is this happening to me? I wondered. What have I done to deserve it? But this perspective was ludicrous. Did I think my life had been mapped out by the gods and that I had played no part in it? Was I being self-indulgent? Was I exaggerating my plight? I asked myself why I was allowing this to happen to me, why this one aspect of my life should ruin everything. Then one day something clicked inside me. I was watching the news and there had been an earthquake in Ecuador. There were pictures of children sitting on the floor and colouring in. Their homes had been razed to the ground but amazingly they carried on with their lives. The devastation was horrendous to see, and certainly put my situation into perspective. But the humanity stayed with me. The strength of character these people were showing was inspirational and humbling. I now felt that it was my turn to fight back.

'There were pictures of children sitting on the floor and colouring in. Their homes had been razed to the ground but amazingly they carried on with their lives.'

I bought a book on motivation in an attempt to find inspiration. My hopes weren't high at the time but it helped. It wasn't a great book, it just resonated with me. It was the guidance that I needed. I think, deep down, I always knew I could do it, but I had an abundance of self-doubt. And that's a massive obstacle to overcome. To get back on my feet, I had to play a role rather than be myself. And I had to find my inner professionalism and my 'weapons' for the battle that lay ahead. Playing the role enabled me to distance myself from my problems. Faith in myself comes and goes. It expands and retracts, depending on the situation, and often shrinks when there is more of the inner me in how I present myself. I have a tendency at times to become the person I hate, or at least the person I really don't want to be. Playing the role helped me to address the problem from someone else's perspective. Anything I would typically struggle to achieve, the professional me in the role would excel in.

The new me was now starting to show potential. I remember listening to a song at the time and although I'd heard it many times before I felt I was hearing it for the first time because I listened closely to the lyrics. The line goes, 'This is the first day of the rest of your life' (*First Day* by Terry Devine-King and Mark Long) and it really hit home for me. I felt like a teenager again, focusing on song lyrics and noting how relevant they were to my life. I began to see things differently and it changed my perspective. I also became more open to the emotional influence of music. I never felt I could just do something spontaneously, but from that moment on my whole outlook changed. And I knew it was going to be significant. Change was now in my power and everything that had happened until this point became irrelevant. A clean sheet, a new beginning, a new life story. This truly was my 'first day,' I thought. Just because it's been that way in the past, doesn't mean that is how it will always be.

As I reflected on my life, events developed new meaning. We are often frightened of change because we don't know how things will turn out, but we should embrace it because not knowing is actually part of the fun. We have so much control in life, sometimes we just need to grasp it with both hands. I also began to wonder if I could have better prepared for my situation. Could I have been mentally ready for such a radical change in my lifestyle? Why was I clinging on to the past so much? The fun and the excitement of the future is that we do not know how things will turn out so we can immerse ourselves in situations and see what develops. I compared this to a film – would I go and see a film that I knew the ending of? Perhaps, if it was a favourite of mine, but in general the answer would be no. The fun of the anticipation has been taken away.

'Just because it's been that way in the past, doesn't mean that is how it will always be.'

In the *Truman Show*, Jim Carrey's character is stuck in a world where his day plays over and over. That would be me, I thought, if I tried to hold on to my lifestyle. We think we don't like change, but it brings excitement, adventure, and something new to our lives. Why do we cling onto things when we've seen change all our lives? Do we become more entrenched in our comfort zones as we get older?

After my redundancy, and my downward spiral of destruction, I came to the conclusion that refusing to change and denying progress is unhealthy. So, I picked myself up, dusted myself down, and decided to put the past behind me. I yearned to make new memories and to deal with challenging situations in a much more productive way. My motto became, 'if change happens, embrace it.' This was difficult because it went against the grain for me. I needed to transform my personality and my strength came from three things that I shall summarise below:

1   Change is normal, change is good, it has happened throughout my life. Stability is just the point at which the former change became established. My life existed before this role and it will continue afterwards.
2   My refusal to let failure define me. Why is this more important than identifying our potential?
3   The Ecuadorian earthquake, and the amazing strength of its survivors, provided context: why have I allowed such a comparatively small change to my life to impact with such magnitude?

Once I had arrived at the decision to try again, I felt great. A weight was lifted from my shoulders and I was ready to tackle the world again. Although I was getting stronger, I knew I would need help so I emailed my friend Carwyn who works in another college. Unfortunately, they don't have a media studies department so I couldn't even find a way in there as a volunteer. But he did agree to meet with me to offer support. I appreciated this as I knew from my own former role just how busy he was.

'We have so much control in life, sometimes we just need to grasp it with both hands.'

Carwyn recommended that I start looking for jobs immediately and that I should widen my scope to include non-teaching jobs. This was part of his initial strategy to get me back on my feet. 'Work breeds work,' he would say, just like my old nan used to. 'But more importantly, you need a focus, a drive, something to get you out of bed every day. And I don't just mean the rude awakening from the dustmen on Wednesday.' We laughed about the reference to the Blur song (Parklife) and that eased my anxiety. I was nervous about doing this because I thought Carwyn would be disappointed in me for having let myself fall to this depth. I guess I was embarrassed as well and felt that he would perceive me as weak. He didn't, though, he was totally understanding. I guess I forgot about all the reasons why he is such an amazing lecturer and why his students love him so much – he is a fantastic person. Great teachers are empathetic and supportive of others' needs. They are also strong in character because they have to be strong for others, such as their students.

Carwyn helped me to get a job in a bar at the weekends and I used this to structure my routine. It was just two nights a week but I knew that it would come round quickly so I couldn't afford to waste time in the week. From hereon, we met up several times over the coming months. Sometimes he came to my house for dinner and we shared a bottle of wine, whilst other times we would just meet up for a coffee and a chat. I also took presents over for his children one time and we sat in his study for hours, debating the purpose of education and discussing character motivations in our favourite films (Carwyn is a psychology lecturer but a film buff in his spare time). I owe Carwyn so much because this shifted my perspective even more. And with my newfound inner drive urging me to get out there and make an impression on the world I secured a lecturing job in a college.

The present

Four years on, I'm now the head of a film and media studies department and I'm the course leader for a film studies course. I have been able to pick up with the networks that I was previously engaged with and have written several more articles for the online magazines. The difference is, however, in my head. I no longer fear change because I know that it doesn't mean failure. And it doesn't mean the end of something entirely if we don't want it to. I have also broadened my approach to life and I have so much more going on than just film studies. I am still passionate about it, but my spare time is taken up with playing the violin (a surprise for me, actually, but something I had long yearned to do). I have friends over regularly and recently competed in a 5K run, and I'm also a governor for a local school. I think my old self would never have believed that I could have achieved so much with my busy career.

I guess that if I was to take a message from all this it would be that there needs to be a balance between what we do and who we are, with time in the middle to live a little. In retrospect, I think I should have had just that little bit of something more in reserve. I should have found times to step away from my career to pursue other interests. I didn't realise it but I was burnt out by the time I was made redundant. In a strange sort of way, and obviously this is retrospective thinking with clarity and objectivity, losing my job helped me to discover other important areas in life, such as my health. Whilst it is admirable to immerse yourself entirely in your career, it is also advisable to keep something back.

'I no longer fear change because I know that it doesn't mean failure.'

Prioritising the important things in life

I met Shanika about eighteen months ago and there have already been several conversations about marriage. Who knows? Maybe one day we will tie the knot. We enjoy each other's company a lot, and we have so much going on in our own lives that there is little time to stop and stress. The film world is still important to me (and I'm still playing the violin) but other things matter too. I think this has even enabled me to become a better lecturer. My students certainly seem to be more content this year. What is probably most important for me now is that I feel more prepared for change. I also don't think that any change would have the same impact on me again because there are so many facets to my life that it is unlikely for all of these to be affected at once. My job may be at stake, my relationship with Shanika might end, I could be prevented from travelling to conferences for whatever reason, I may no longer be in a position to write for the magazines etc., but it is unlikely that all these things will happen together, and that for me is a key part of developing resilience.

'So, I picked myself up, dusted myself down, and decided to put the past behind me.'

11 Case study

Amelie's story

As I have worked in FE for a number of years in different roles, I was recently asked to write a case study reflecting on my resilience. I don't consider myself to be a particularly resilient person; I think we all go through difficult times, and stress is by no means unique to any individual. But I have had quite a few, shall we say, unfortunate incidents in my life that have probably made me the person I am today. I think it is good to draw on your past to shape you as these are important life experiences. We never know what is round the next corner, but we do know what was round the several corners before this one because we have already experienced them. Whatever we do in life it can be meaningful in a variety of ways, even though at the time we are probably unaware of any significance. We can also learn from other people's experiences and my opinion is that in the Western world this is something we do not do enough of. So here is my story, make of it what you will.

I was very much an ordinary kid growing up, although we moved home a lot. My father was a high-flying sales executive and he had had several jobs before I was 7 years old. By the time of my second move (and third different school), I was beginning to get the picture – don't get close to your friends because you might be leaving them soon. This was hard to handle at first and it probably put me closer to my mum and dad. They were amazing parents, and even though Dad had this career that took him across the country he always had time for me and my sister Fleur. He picked us up from school every Thursday and took us to the park. I remember spending hours in that park and at weekends he was always keen to take us on an adventure. How he did this still amazes me. He had a really busy lifestyle and he was always working on a project for some company. He was a senior manager and shareholder of a company that provided equipment for offices. But instead of working for the central office, he would get assigned to an area of the country to develop one of the local branches.

During his career, Dad had also written several books on sales and marketing. But he never failed to have time for his family, and he always made both Fleur and I feel special. This helped with the house moves and I think we just got used to not developing any real bond with an area or the people in it. I believe this has also helped me today as I have always followed my career, regardless of

DOI: 10.4324/9780367824211-14

where in the country it takes me. I've never been tied to a location and I would even consider moving abroad to work if the opportunity was there.

Apart from the moves, it was the perfect home life for me as a child. Or at least I thought it was. Just after my eighth birthday, Dad developed lung cancer. He didn't even smoke which I later thought was yet another kick in the teeth. We didn't know anything about it at the time because Mum and Dad carried on as normal. One day, around six months later, I caught Mum sobbing in her bedroom. As I went to comfort her, she immediately responded with a smile. She reassured me that they were tears of happiness and that she was happy because she loved us so much and felt really lucky to have this wonderful family. I didn't know any better so I accepted it, but what she was really crying over was that the cancer had metastasized and Dad only had months to live. She wouldn't tell me this because my dad had asked her not to. 'Let's live a normal life for as much as we possibly can,' he said. 'I don't want this to ruin my time with my family.'

Dad was the epitome of resilience and if only 10% of his strength has rubbed off on me I will consider myself proud and thankful. 'I just love seeing my family happy,' he told Mum. He died two weeks before Christmas and just four days after my ninth birthday. I'll never forget this birthday. About a month before, Dad had pulled out all the stops and he took us to Lapland for a few days. He'd been saving up for it all year which was a much bigger gesture than I realised because I now know that he had been paying for treatment too. I think he knew that this would be the last opportunity to do something significant with his daughters and it must have been eating him up inside. But I never saw any signs of this, and even though I was only nine I believe I would have known if something was amiss because there came a time when it could no longer be hidden. Dad was at home and severely ill. He had lost a lot of weight and 'the talk' finally came. I won't go into the details, and even now I am crying as I write this; suffice to say it wasn't pleasant.

> 'Dad was the epitome of resilience and if only 10% of his strength has rubbed off on me I will consider myself proud and thankful.'

Strangely, I became strong from this experience. I vowed to fight back at life. I was angry and confused and I had a lot of pent-up emotion. Mum had become strong too and she took to raising us on her own. I can honestly say that my parents have been the biggest influence in my life because there have been numerous times – even when I reached my 30s – that I could have given up on everything and stopped believing that things will improve. I carry a picture of Dad in my purse. I look at it when I'm feeling sad and it makes me happy. And I look at it when I'm feeling happy and it makes me sad. It's difficult to describe the emotional journey this picture takes me on. The only consistency is when I use it motivate myself. If I called Mum when I was feeling down, she knew that merely starting the sentence with 'if Dad was here …' was enough to give me a push in the right direction. I owe it to Dad to succeed. He and Mum made me what I am.

Teaching

I graduated with a 2i in Sociology and went immediately onto a PGCE in Post-Compulsory Education and Training. I think I always wanted to teach as I wanted to give something back. You might wonder why, given my traumatic upbringing, but when you have life experiences you should share these with others. Some may feel that they have had better childhoods than mine because both their parents were there for them growing up. I would disagree with this. For me, my childhood was fantastic, and the only downside was that it had to end at nine years old. I grew up fast after Dad passed away, because I had to. And because Mum needed me. This meant that my sister could still enjoy her childhood and we could each look after her in our own way. Fleur was just four when Dad died so she doesn't recall much. Mum did her absolute best to make up for Dad going. And I always looked out for my little sister so I had to be tough for both of us. Mum, of course, was tough for the whole family.

So, we grew up well and despite Dad being stolen from us I felt privileged. Training to be a teacher was my way of giving something back and helping others to fulfil their dreams. But I wasn't giving back to replicate my own learning experience because that had been fraught with disaster too. The teacher who most inspired me to become a teacher was a horrible, miserable, sadistic individual who clearly resented everyone he came across. He was an awful man and an even worse teacher. He taught maths in my high school and most of the kids failed it. Maths is difficult enough without someone like this. He particularly despised me for some reason – I have no idea what that reason was – and he offered very little help.

> 'The teacher who most inspired me to become a teacher was a horrible, miserable, sadistic individual who clearly resented everyone he came across.'

Fortunately, he didn't know me because acting like this towards me only made me stronger. And Mum was good at maths so she would explain things to me. She complained a number of times to the school but back then it was different and schools supported the staff regardless of how good or bad they were. Clearly, in the eyes of those running the school, we were just trouble-makers who complained. But they never put two and two together to see that we had a wonderful opinion of the teaching in other subject areas, it was just maths. Or more to the point, it was just that particular maths teacher. He seemed to want to bring me down. By the time Fleur arrived at the school he was gone so we felt lucky that we had managed to shield her yet again. I'm not sure that we always did the right thing for her, though, as she's not very resilient these days. She still comes to me when she is stressed, or if things become a little too difficult for her, and she is married with two children of her own. Most of the time her so-called difficulties are minor and I wonder if sheltering her was the best thing to do.

As a teacher, I wanted to change lives in a positive way. My maths teacher inspired me in his poor, unprofessional way and also indirectly helped me to build resilience. I don't recommend this for others, but I do think that learning from bad experiences is important. There are many things in life we cannot change, but we can change how they affect us.

After completing the PGCE, my first teaching role was in a small college in the north of England. I was teaching sociology which was amazing because these positions don't come up very often. I guess I was lucky but in other ways it was my determination that got me into that position. I had completed my teacher training placement there and they were really impressed with me. I did some sessional work and covered some of the psychology classes (not my strength but I filled a gap) and functional skills because my maths and English skills are strong (despite the experiences with my former maths teacher). The sociology lecturer left to have a baby so I took over from her. I later became permanent when she announced that she would be extending her maternity and taking a career break to raise her child. I was young – still in my twenties – yet progressing well in my career. I had recently moved in with my boyfriend; things were going well and Mum was happy. All was well with the world.

> 'There are many things in life we cannot change, but we can change how they affect us.'

But then it happened ...

The second major tragedy to befall my erratic existence. Mum was driving home one evening after visiting my sister's house. As she was nearing the end of the motorway, she slowed down for a roundabout. A drunk driver smashed into the back of her car at over 80 miles per hour. The girl who was driving had been to a party and was nearly four times over the limit. She had fallen asleep at the wheel. The impact caused Mum's car to spin and then flip over several times, coming to an eventual stop on its roof. Mum was rushed into hospital with her injuries, and we were told from the outset that it didn't look good. Mum had spinal injuries and she only had a 50–50 chance of survival. And if she did pull through, it was very likely she would be paralysed from the accident. And the drunk driver? Minor injuries. Minor! Why does she get to walk away from this? I asked Fleur, frantically pacing round the waiting area. I'm not vindictive as a rule but I just couldn't hold this in.

We never slept that night. In fact, we didn't go home at all. But that made very little difference to the outcome. Mum passed away from her injuries at 04:03. My life had been turned upside down once again and I prayed to Dad for strength. My sister was distraught and looking back I think I only held things together to keep her on track. She needed me more than ever. I could have been selfish and demanded the attention, particularly as she had not really suffered with losing Dad. But the way I saw it, I was the eldest and I had been in a better position because I had memories with both my parents. So I remained the strong one. That is, until about nine months later when I finally broke down. I needed the release because I had bottled it up for such a long time. I knew that I would have to come back from this but the feeling of starting again – and not even from the beginning because I was in a much worse position now – destroyed me. I shut myself away for over a week. Fleur never seemed to notice as we sometimes go for two or three weeks without talking because of our busy jobs.

Whenever I'm faced with a situation like this, I have to think and think and think until my head hurts. I probably overthink things – I must have asked myself a million times why it happened – but it's my way of dealing with the situation. I have to be in control and I have to have all the information to hand. I sit, I reflect, and I plan. Intersperse these three activities with lots of weeping and you have my recipe for resilience. I accept that it's not earth-shattering, but it works for me. I think the key part is the control – what can I do and how can I do it? And importantly, what can't I do and why can't I do it? My final thought process is based on how I will achieve my objectives and how my plan can be put into action. This is also significant because this is the point at which I open up my thought processes to the help and support that is around me. I no longer have my parents but there are friends and work colleagues and even professional help if I need it.

> 'Whenever I'm faced with a situation like this, I have to think and think and think until my head hurts.'

A plan is formed and then I emerge from my week-long cocoon, ready to work with the key figures who will play a role. I don't recommend this strategy for everyone as the isolation is tough. But it's how I deal with things. I do need the company of other people, but when I need to reflect I feel that nobody is an adequate substitute for Mum and Dad. Whilst alone, I approach my problems from their perspective. I try to think like they would. Even if I can't actually do this, it makes me feel we're connected. Nothing will ever bring Mum and Dad back, but I will also never forget them. Reflecting as I write this, I think I am trying to be the best person I possibly can so they can be proud of me.

When Dad passed away, my religion helped me a lot, and I knew he was looking down on me every day, willing me to succeed. How could I possibly let him down? I had to fight. I feel that Dad gave up his life to make us happy and his strength helped to build my own resilience. Seeing his picture is a powerful reminder of his love and commitment to our family. I have had many traumatic experiences in my life but I always feel that Mum and Dad are by my side. I stop and reflect for a minute and then I feel them next to me. It helps me to go on.

Strike three

They say things come in threes and around five years after Mum died I started to believe this was true. CJ, my boyfriend at the time, had asked me to marry him. Four years after we lost Mum we got married. I was barely functioning but trying as much as I could to put my life back into some normality. The tragedy of Mum had hit me late and even though they say time is a healer, in my experience the pain might fade a little but it never goes away. There were now two huge chunks of my inner self that had been ripped out of me, the wounds refusing to heal. But I found I could move on to some extent, probably because I had to. I was distraught but was slowly growing stronger each day. We had a new life on the way so I was aware that my priorities would change; I had to be strong for the child.

Just two years into our marriage, however, and I now found myself the pregnant victim of a cheat. And no ordinary cheat at that. My so-called husband was planning to marry someone else and I knew nothing at all of this until I accidentally found a credit card statement with a Paris hotel bill on it. I checked the dates and it was the weekend he was at a training event for his job. CJ was an IT consultant and he was supposed to be attending some Microsoft convention. Unlike the pain, the details escape me. *How could you do that to your unborn child?* I did some digging and discovered more unusual payments and gifts such as jewellery and expensive perfumes ordered that I know I never received.

I knew it was over and far from holding in there and 'trying to make it work' I shut him out my life. I needed to do this, I needed to stay in control. I was determined that his pettiness and infidelity would not hurt me any more than was necessary. I had already been hurt most of my life. I knew pain and as tragic as it is when relationships break up the feeling would never compare to my true losses. I refused to expend any energy on a man who didn't want me, a man who put his own selfish desires before a beautiful family. Strike three, I thought, determined to get through it.

Now

After juggling a hectic lifestyle of bringing Denzel up on my own and trying to fit in a career (I also started an MA through the Open University), I think I've done a pretty good job. Denzel is 13 and is doing well at school whilst I am the principal of my college. I achieved this position through hard work (and probably a bit of luck) but for the most part it was my refusal to give up. Yes, I've had my moments and believe me I have weakened incredibly at times. But I think resilience is about carrying on, whatever you're facing. It is often about starting again, even when you are at rock-bottom. But being at the bottom is OK because you can only go up. And when it comes to progress, we should look to the future and not the past. To me, the past is something to reflect on, to relive the good times through my memories. It is not something that I would wish to shape my future. I can't change anything that's happened to me, although of course I would if I could. But what I can do is to set myself on the right path in life.

If life pushes you off track, jump back on. I don't feel that I have any right to be miserable. Dad continued for as long as he could, smiling every day and telling us he loved us whilst a horrible disease ate away at him. So, I owe it to him to carry on. I owe it to him to be happy. And I owe it to him to make something of my life in order to, at the very least, acknowledge his sacrifices. I also owe it to Mum to cope, to show her that I am a strong and independent individual. I believe we have a lot of control over our own destiny and we should work on that as much as we can. The things you can't control in life will happen anyway, so why worry about them? Don't concern yourself with trying to change the unchangeable.

'If life pushes you off track, jump back on.'

I know the world is full of wrongs, but I also know that there is little I can do to effect any major changes. But I can play my part and I believe that's crucial. If we all played our part, then the impact would be significant. Collectively, we can make an impression on the world, and as teachers we should help people develop into fantastic and learned individuals. I came into teaching to give something back, even though you could argue I have lost more than I have gained. I don't see it that way, however. Both Mum and Dad were amazing people and I was lucky to have had them in my life. As well as parents, they were role models, they were mentors, they were teachers. They guided me in life. Now, it is my turn to guide others and I know that even if people don't work together enough, there is one thing I can do: I can control my world. In my world, you get to do the things you want as long as you put in the time, energy and commitment. You get to go to the places you want as long as you do everything in your power to make it happen. And you get to make a contribution, however small, to someone's life. I can control my world so I will continue to do so for as long as I possibly can.

12 Case study

Shanice's story

I've never been one for multitasking. I looked into it and was surprised to discover that it doesn't work. If that's true, it's a great finding for me because I like to focus on one thing and really do it well. Multitasking always feels like I'm diluting my focus, doing something half-heartedly. People remember you for what you do and if it's only one thing, but it is something that is absolutely exceptional, then that is far more powerful than spreading yourself thinly. Margaret Mitchell was a famous novelist but if you ask the average person what she wrote they are unlikely to go beyond *Gone with the Wind*. In many ways, no other works matter because it was that particular novel that really put her on the map of the literary world. *Gone with the Wind* is regarded as a classic (probably because it was made into a film that has stood the test of time) and as people are still aware of it over 80 years later, it is clearly a fantastic achievement. I don't say this to comment on the issues raised in the film, merely to show that its overall strength lies in its longevity. (My mum is also a fan as the screen adaptation is her favourite film.)

To-do lists

Do something well and it will be worthwhile. Do something poorly and you needn't have bothered. I truly believe that. I think we all want to be remembered for something outstanding that we've done or achieved, so quality not quantity is the key phrase here. But how does this relate to my story of resilience? I believe that focusing on a particular task can help us to fight back when we need to get our life back on track. Setting daily goals keeps me going and whenever I am going through a difficult time in my life, I lean on my to-do lists. I feel I should warn you, however. My approach can be counterproductive to resilience for some people as it places pressure on one thing at a time, so you may need to monitor it. Make sure that what you are dealing with is not causing you more stress. However, it works for me and I believe it actually contributes to my resilience.

Firstly, I like to have a focus. To-do lists are important but they have to be used effectively. For me, there's no point just putting down a list of items that I would *like* to tick off. I need to note down the items that I *will* do. So, 'list' is probably the wrong word as it suggests you need to have several items down

DOI: 10.4324/9780367824211-15

there and tick them off as you progress. That's a nice idea, and it works if it comprises simple tasks – send off a birthday card to a friend or mop the kitchen floor and so on – but for more onerous tasks, such as goals, you need to be realistic. Sometimes it is necessary to note everything down which needs attending to so that it doesn't slip from your mind. That's also fine so long as the list doesn't trail along the floor as you're holding it. I don't like it because it either reminds me of what I still have to do, and that puts pressure on me. Having said this, if I do feel it necessary to have long to-do lists then I will break them up into the time I intend to spend on each one, such as into days and even weeks.

> 'Do something well and it will be worthwhile. Do something poorly and you needn't have bothered.'

I do have my main to-do list – the long one with everything I can think of on it (this one does trail along the floor) – but I don't work directly off this. The shorter ones are based on how long I need to tick off every item. Usually, I have a to-do list for each day and a larger one for the week, and each item is taken from my main to-do list. This might sound like it's cumbersome, but it works for me. It also helps me to compartmentalise and prioritise the main list if it is overwhelming. Daily lists always seem more doable. It is also worth mentioning here that some days I challenge myself (and if an item is not finished it can move over to the next day) but other days I give myself a break. I might have an 'easy' day, wherein I can easily achieve all the points. This is good because it gives me a boost in confidence to tackle the more challenging ones. Another trick I like to use is to cross off the easy ones first as I get a real sense of achievement from this. Just two hours into my day I can be well over halfway through the list.

I work through my to-do list in a systematic manner which is why I like to list things in order of how I will address them. I like to focus my attention on just one of the items and forget about the others as I work through this parti-cular one to the best of my ability. I need it to be good because I want to truly say I have achieved it and not just paid lip service to it. It is tempting to tick something off when I have worked on it, but if I have not addressed it fully then I will refrain from scratching it off. My concentration for each is intense and my sole focus is to undertake whatever is needed in order to be satisfied that I have met that particular item.

When I get into a task from my to-do list, I like to approach it thoroughly. I'm talking about big tasks, of course, such as revising a module for my teach-ing. It's sometimes difficult to do this because there are other things that need to be done, but for me it's about doing it well – making sure that I've paid attention to detail and that I haven't skimped on the quality of my work. If I cannot spend the time I need on it, I go back to the more pressing ones and get those ticked off to give me some head space.

I'm quite a committed person so I insist on seeing things through to the end. I don't entertain failure unless I absolutely have to, and even then it's only because things are out of my control. Most things in life are achievable, I believe, as long as you bide your time and stick at it. At least, that is what I have found works for me. If something doesn't happen in the way I plan it, perseverance is crucial. I keep at it because I usually arrive in the end, even if the route is a lot different from what I had planned. All roads lead to Rome, as they say. Once you get where you want to be, or do what you really want to do, it doesn't matter how you got there.

Drawing from experience

When I left university, I wanted to do an MA in English but I hit a financial barrier. The bank promised a loan over the phone but then reneged in person because I didn't have a job to go to at the end. I withdrew from the course and reverted to my Plan B: defer and work for a year to save up the fees. Plan B then became Plan C, or whatever name you wish to give it because it wasn't my plan at all by then, and I got swept along with earning a living, particularly as I was promoted in my job to restaurant manager. I loved it but I wasn't convinced it was ultimately for me. The following year I left to pursue the MA full time and that had been a really difficult decision to make. I knew I would be leaving the comfort and security of decently paid employment, and what little savings I had would go towards the fees.

> 'My stubbornness said persist, but I found it difficult to keep positive.'

I thought about the bank adviser's comment about guaranteed employment and it made me nervous. I became anxious over my insecure future and the stress was unbearable. I had always been a fighter, but I suddenly felt I was losing this battle. My stubbornness said persist, but I found it difficult to keep positive. Putting things into perspective was difficult for me and I really had to draw on all my reserves of resilience to continue. Inside, I truly believed that I was going to do something wonderful with my passion for English and language. But in my mind, I grappled with the reality of my situation. The literary world is a competitive one and as much faith as I had in myself, I started to doubt whether success would ever be mine. But then, I wasn't even sure what I was judging success on. I think I just needed to be content in a career. Things happen for a reason, I always feel, and I knew that my experiences would one day been meaningful. The MA was a challenge and I was tempted numerous times to give up. But I didn't because something inside was driving me. When I try to pinpoint where this resilience came from, I think back to my childhood.

As a family, we had very little in the way of luxuries. We were what is now known as 'of low socioeconomic status,' but what we termed back then as just 'poor.' We couldn't afford things that other families could afford – fancy shoes, expensive coats, designer labels – and we never had a colour television until I was about 12. We certainly never had a car. We walked everywhere; public transport was our luxury. On the odd occasion we did get on a bus, my brother and I would run upstairs and try and get to the front so we could steer the bus using the long bar across the windscreen. As we looked down at the people at the bus stop, we imagined we were doing a really important job in chauffeuring all the people around. Life was tough so in many ways *we* became tough as we hardened to our situation. But we always tried to see the best in everything. I think we had to. When you're used to having nothing, you don't really crave anything; and when you are at the bottom every achievement is a bonus. But what a great feeling each one is. I started to see that I could better myself through achievement as I didn't really have career aspirations before that. Consequently, I became the first (and last so far) in my family to go to university. I learnt that success is not something that is handed down to us, it is something we achieve through hard work.

I attribute my resilience to my upbringing, then. Times were tough so we were always prepared for hardship. This put things into perspective for me and established my outlook on life. Life was difficult but for us that was just how it was. But even those with fame and fortune experience their share of tragedies. We imagine the stars have it made in life, we imagine that their lives have been amazing and straightforward – striding along from one success story to the next, with luck seeming to ooze out of their ears. But lots of stars lead tragic lives, and I believe they become successful because they can overcome adversity. Many face extreme difficulties in life yet pull through, sometimes becoming even stronger. I don't know the stats on this sort of thing, but I have read a lot of autobiographies of famous people and there is usually something to admire about how they've handled things in their lives. I guess this is resilience: getting up when you've been knocked down and facing your fears again, knowing that you may well be knocked down again and again yet refusing to give up. I think this is why my experiences as a child helped me.

> 'Success is not something that is handed down to us, it is something we achieve through hard work.'

I have experienced rejection many times in my life and seemed to have had more than my fair share of failures, so I am no longer intimidated by any of this. This doesn't mean I no longer care, it doesn't mean I accept fate, it just means I take failure in my stride. And I thought most people did until I came into teaching. Until I moved up the social ladder, so to speak, I thought that most people were resilient because it was a part of life. Not everyone has had a hard life, however, and many crumble at the seemingly little things in life. I think it is wrong to say that the way to build resilience is through a tough upbringing, but I believe that I became resilient because of the difficult situations I faced.

Back to the MA and my academic journey. I really struggled to muster up the self-belief that I would use this degree in the most effective way possible. I had to convince myself that it would open doors and that I should resume the positive approach that had worked well for me in the past. During my study, I gave a talk to some undergrads and I really enjoyed the adult interaction. This is it, I thought: teaching! I loved my subject and being able to engage with it more was an exciting prospect. I knew from this point that teaching adults was to be my metier. So, I looked into FE and since then I have never looked back. I love helping others and teaching is so rewarding. Perhaps, because I experienced bad times as a child yet survived and flourished, teaching is my way of giving something back: helping others to survive their experiences.

> 'I guess this is resilience: getting up when you've been knocked down and facing your fears again, knowing that you may well be knocked down again and again yet refusing to give up.'

Resilience for success

We often impose restrictions on ourselves, and whilst overly adventurous ideas might challenge reality, many of us exercise too much self-constraint. Far from aspiring to be the next prime minister, we sometimes struggle to believe that we will even land a job. But we should push these thoughts aside and resist allowing them to destroy us. We develop resilience from our experiences, and we draw on these to face our challenges, although it's difficult when there is a mismatch between our experiences and what we currently face. How do you deal with being overworked when in all your previous jobs the workload was fine? To address this, you have to think outside the box, and I have a little strategy for doing so. I believe we have a wealth of resources to draw on and just need to find them. To do this, we may need to relate alternative, and even seemingly unconnected, experiences to what we are facing. And then we need to use this connection to conjure up confidence and strength for our new situation. After all, the emotions are the same so we at least have a starting point.

Like most people, I know what it's like to lose a loved one (when I lost my granddad it hit me hard), and I'm aware that emotional bruising will eventually heal. This didn't make the situation any better, and I still needed to grieve, but it gave me resilience for the next time. Obviously, I don't want to relive the experience, or conjure up those horrific emotions I felt, but I am able to utilise the experience in a positive way. I do this by accepting the basic parts of the process, such as the following:

- Grieving is necessary but things get better
- My emotional condition makes me sad but there are happy moments (memories)
- Suffering is normal but it is temporary
- Change is inevitable (death = change) and life goes on
- We eventually return to our former selves

This is something I have been trialling with in my experiences and below is an example of how I utilised it.

Applying distance

About five years ago I bought a new house. My mortgage payments were high but I accepted this as it was my dream home. I had always worked hard in life so I wanted to be rewarded. I had to do a lot of work on the house so I was careful with my spending. But I still ran up a lot of debts on credit cards. After about a year in the house, and with debts pushing £20,000, I suddenly found myself facing redundancy. I couldn't believe what was happening to me. I had felt secure in my job (I actually thought it would see me to retirement) and now it was about to end. My stress levels were at an all-time high and I didn't know what to do. My options to move to another college also weren't looking good. It was a bad time of year and with the latest rounds of funding cuts there was an abundance of lecturers applying for the same small number of vacancies. Because of my financial commitments (debts), I only had a limited amount of time to get another job. I was also quite pessimistic at this point and found it hard to see a way forward; thoughts of losing my house were consuming me. The only option was to look at the situation from a different angle.

I won't go into the unnecessary financial details of how you can get through a situation such as this – e.g. mortgage holidays, interest-only rates, consolidating debts or even taking in a lodger – as this advice is already out there. What I would like to focus on is the effect this stress had on me, and how I dealt with the emotional turmoil. Whilst it is right to reflect on the employment situation, I couldn't assume that I wouldn't get a job again because that was not a definite outcome. Having had several jobs in the sector I knew from experience that one job did not define me. I also knew that there are many financial support mechanisms that I could draw on to alleviate the financial burden, even if they were temporary. Many people can, and do, lose their homes so this was obviously a real threat. But some unfortunately do so because they are ill-equipped or struggle to cope with the stress and anxiety that this type of situation generates.

Depression and loss of focus is understandable from a compassionate perspective, but for me I had to find a way out, and I needed a comparable experience to draw on. It seemed wrong to allow this situation to destroy me when I had moved on from the loss of my granddad, so I challenged the impact it was having on me. I denied its effect because I believed that accepting it would be a betrayal to the passing of my granddad. If I was to become upset it would have to be directed at the fact that my granddad was no longer in my life. As for the debts, I was concerned about how they could be paid off, but I refused to worry about them or to allow them to take control of my life.

The effects of worrying

Worrying might seem like a realistic perspective, but for me it is crossing the bridge before I've arrived. It adds stress to the situation if I fixate on either the worst-case scenario or an unwanted outcome. I like to spend time thinking about my concern so I understand it better, but this can turn to worrying if I'm not conscious of my thought processes. Reflecting on my situation can be productive but worrying is counterproductive. For me, worrying never resolves anything for me. It is anxiety-induced thinking that is misguided because it is clouded in negativity. Therefore, I always aim to push it out of my head. This is easier said than done, but when I feel that worry is starting to dominate my thinking, I focus on something unrelated until I take back control

> 'Worrying never resolves anything for me. It is anxiety-induced thinking that is misguided because it is clouded in negativity.'

I have found from experience that worrying causes the situation to deteriorate as it encourages negative self-fulfilling prophecies to manifest. I emphasise this point because I differentiate worrying from immersive thinking and evaluative reflection. If my concerns are thought through, and I seek ways to resolve the situation, I would never call this 'worrying.' Also, however a situation turns out, worrying doesn't contribute anything. For instance, supposing you find yourself distracted when driving past a speed camera. You panic and start to worry that you have inadvertently gone over the speed limit at precisely the wrong time. Perhaps you reflect on the impact of this – points on your licence, an increase in your insurance premium and so on – and it causes you to become anxious as you await the outcome. After four weeks of stressing, you finally realise that you're in the clear. Result: four weeks of unnecessary stress. But let's imagine you were unfortunate enough to have received the fine. Did the worrying prevent it from happening? Result: four weeks of unnecessary stress.

In conclusion, my resilience has developed from my experiences in life and it has often helped me get through traumatic times. It also helped me to get back into FE eventually. But I am nothing special in this regard. We all have life experiences that we can draw on, and although we can never be truly prepared, we can have some idea of how we could cope during a stressful time. After all, we can do it for positive situations. You probably already have a plan for what you'd do if you won the lottery.

13 Concluding thoughts

In December 2019, a pandemic emerged in Wuhan, China, but few could predict the impact this would have on the world. Covid-19 quickly spread across the globe and within months there were arguably few people on the earth who had not at least heard of this virus, let alone become aware of its deadly potential. Covid-19 transformed lives in many countries in the world and, at the time of writing, continues to do so.

In March 2020, the World Health Organization (WHO) expressed concern over how Covid-19 was 'generating stress throughout the population' (WHO, 2020, p. 1). For teachers, the profession also took on a new form around this time. Teaching moved online during the second international lockdown and isolation began to take its toll on individuals. Covid-19 impacted widely on the profession, including those training to work in it. For instance, student teachers in FE suddenly found themselves delivering online lessons, some never having stood in front of a class in person. Whilst behavioural concerns were dramatically reduced, however, the pandemic brought new challenges

Teachers were now faced with a new reality, and even though many felt they were au fait with the benefits of technology-enhanced learning, few could predict the negative impact of the social isolation of the new online learning. Resilience grew in importance and teachers were faced with additional workloads as they familiarised themselves with delivering teaching online and thus adapting resources. Responses to the new way of teaching were mixed. For some, teaching online prompted creativity and encouraged fresh engagement, even for teachers of practical subjects such as drama and sports. For others, however, the challenge was unfulfilling and merely perceived as a barrier to learning. Those with little resilience arguably found such a dramatic shift in teaching to be overwhelming, but the situation could easily have been deconstructed to illustrate that its component parts are in themselves easy to handle. Teaching online was not a new concept but it challenged conformity and it presented the need for change. Those who seemingly coped more effectively displayed positive attitudes and were able to reconceptualise the problem as a hurdle rather than a barrier (see Chapter 5).

DOI: 10.4324/9780367824211-16

Where do we go from here?

The modern teacher is required to be flexible and adaptable. Change is often inevitable and predicting the future seems no easier today than it did two decades ago. If anything, the world is moving faster in today's society and technology and advances in science are shifting the way we think and the way we function. Cultural attitudes and behaviours are also in danger of shifting as they evolve in response to the change in circumstances, and the resilient teacher should be aware of the importance of being ready to adapt. If we believe that change is inevitable then we may be able to deal with it more efficiently. Various vaccines have been created in response to Covid-19, but the fight is clearly unfinished. With new strains appearing across the globe and spreading rapidly due to the current global shrinkage effect from cheaper and more available travel options, the world will continue to change and may continue to pose threats to education professionals. There is a high probability, then, that the non-resilient teacher will struggle to survive in the modern education world. Resilience is essential for teachers because teaching is about growth, and growth cannot occur without change. Resilience, then, supports education professionals to continue doing what they do best, even when the odds are against them.

Reference

WHO (2020). Mental health and psychosocial considerations during the COVID-19 outbreak. Geneva: World Health Organization. https://www.who.int/docs/default-source/coronaviruse/mental-health-considerations.pdf

Index